The Pentecost Paradigm

The Pentecost Paradigm

Ten Strategies for Becoming
a Multiracial Congregation

Jacqueline J. Lewis
and John Janka

WESTMINSTER
JOHN KNOX PRESS
LOUISVILLE · KENTUCKY

First edition
Published by Westminster John Knox Press
Louisville, Kentucky

18 19 20 21 22 23 24 25 26 27—10 9 8 7 6 5 4 3 2

Unless otherwise indicated, Scripture quotations are from the New Revised Standard Version of the Bible, copyright © 1989 by the Division of Christian Education of the National Council of the Churches of Christ in the U.S.A., and are used by permission.

Book design by Sharon Adams
Cover design by Mary Ann Smith

Library of Congress Cataloging-in-Publication Data

Names: Lewis, Jacqueline Janette, 1959- author. | Janka, John, author.
Title: The Pentecost paradigm : ten strategies for becoming a multiracial
  congregation / Jacqueline J. Lewis and John Janka.
Description: Louisville, KY : Westminster John Knox Press, 2018. |
  Identifiers: LCCN 2017050179 (print) | LCCN 2017052513 (ebook) | ISBN
  9781611648553 (ebk.) | ISBN 9780664263386 (pbk. : alk. paper)
Subjects: LCSH: Church. | Cultural fusion. | Pentecost. | Race
  relations--Religious aspects--Christianity.
Classification: LCC BV600.3 (ebook) | LCC BV600.3 .L487 2018 (print) | DDC
  250.89--dc23
LC record available at https://lccn.loc.gov/2017050179

Most Westminster John Knox Press books are available at special quantity discounts when purchased in bulk by corporations, organizations, and special-interest groups. For more information, please e-mail SpecialSales@wjkbooks.com.

For Emma and Richard, who taught me the power of family to navigate the treacherous waters of American racism; for Middle Collegiate Church, whose commitment to revolutionary love inspires me to work for the Reign of God on earth; and for John, my partner and best friend in the struggle for justice.

—Jacqui

For my mother, Florence; and my grandfather John Ecret, who taught me to be open and curious and to embrace the stranger for what they may have to teach me. And for my wife, Jacqueline, who is my life partner and co-conspirator.

—John

Contents

Acknowledgments

*A*long the way, we have had some remarkable teachers. Among them are

the Rev. Jack Gilbert Sr., the Rev. Patti Daley, the Rev. Michael Livingston, and the Rev. Gordon Dragt

Roselia Cobb, Roy Pneuman, Margaret Bruhl, Marie Dixon, and Speed Leas

George Kelsey, James Cone, Arthur Pressley, and Traci West

Michelle Alexander, Jim Kay, Delores Williams, Katie Cannon, and Virgilio Elizondo

Isabel Wilkerson, Ella Baker, Martin Luther King Jr., and Fannie Lou Hamer

Carol Anderson, Tim Wise, Thandeka, Michael Eric Dyson, Barack Hussein Obama, and Miguel de la Torre

Curtiss De Young, Gloria Anzaldua, Toni Morrison, W.E.B. Du Bois, Alice Walker, and Donald Winnicott

Auburn Senior Fellows

Great Uncle George Jordan—Mississippi civil rights activist and babysitter for little Jacqui

Introduction

The fact that you picked up this book to see what it's about is exciting for us. We think multiracial and multicultural congregations are essential to heal the fundamental divisions in our nation. We believe communities of faith must lead the charge against racism and xenophobia. Growing diverse, inclusive congregations requires spiritual imagination, a vision for a healed world, and the willingness to address the ferment underway in our culture. When we worship, pray, and work together in diverse community; when we acknowledge and celebrate our differences; when we stay in relationship and stand together as justice-seeking people, we are modeling the world as God intended it to be.

Why is this important? Racism in America is a virus that infects most of us and impacts all of us. This virus is tenacious and resistant to treatment. We often deny we have this virus or that we have internalized it because facing racism tampers with our self-image, can cause a sense of blame and guilt in us, and requires us to change how we see the world. As a nation, we make strides toward a more perfect union only to watch the virus mutate. It goes underground, reappearing in uncivil discourse, showing up in the ways economic injustice tracks with ethnicity, in the ways the prison population is disproportionately black and brown, in the ways drug laws are written resulting in devastating incarceration rates for people of color, and in the ways policies like "Stop-and-Frisk" and "Stand Your Ground" impact people of color most profoundly. Because the virus is resilient, many of our schools and communities are being segregated again, and many of our housing patterns are also being resegregated.

As a result of immigration and birthrates, demographers anticipate that the United States will have no ethnic majority by 2040. This demographic shift is true not only for this country but also for other currently white-majority European nations as well, as migration patterns change and people are displaced by war, poverty, and oppression. This is both a challenge and an opportunity for all congregations, especially for majority white Christian faith communities. Without the capacity for meaningful engagement with growing diverse populations of color, white congregations will begin to decline by attrition. Many are already experiencing this challenge.

In his book *The End of White Christian America*, Robert P. Jones announces the passing of white Christianity. He observes, "The cause of death was determined to be a combination of environmental and internal factors—complications stemming from major demographic changes in the country, along with religious disaffiliation as many of its younger members began to doubt WCA's continued relevance in a shifting cultural environment."[1] He goes on to name two major issues at play in its demise: its inability to come to terms with its historical

1

failure to effectively address issues of race and its struggle to understand and embrace issues of sexual orientation and gender.

In a culture that has not yet "overcome," we are convinced that our strongest defense against racism—the very best way to build immunity to virulent racial tensions in our nation and address the widening racial, ethnic, and economic divide—is the development of multiracial, multicultural communities of faith. In radically welcoming communities of faith where everyone is welcome just as they are as they come through the door, we can rehearse the reign and shalom of God here and now.

Many congregations of the first century were diverse. Once the movement of Jesus' followers leaped the borders of Jerusalem and then Palestine, it entered a world of remarkable diversity. The early movement had to contend with divisions within itself about whether the Gentiles of the Greek and Roman world even qualified for membership in this movement. This question precipitated a crisis for the church at Antioch, which was culturally diverse and was being told by the elders in Jerusalem that they must first be circumcised and become Jews religiously and culturally before they could be saved and enter into the fellowship of the church. It was left to Peter and Paul to sort this out, and they did, acknowledging that the message of Jesus was for all people equally, not just for the Jews. This led to opening the door to a diverse world eager to hear the good news. Churches established from this point onward often reflected the diversity of their setting and were held together in unity by the faith that was taught and preached.

It was an all too brief period of amazing inclusion of diverse people forming faith communities in this fledgling Christian movement. Its growing prominence led to the co-opting of this fast-growing movement by the Roman Empire, when Constantine found it politically advantageous to become a Christian. This was the beginning of the domestication and "empiring" of Jesus, when his teachings became an instrument of the powerful. When this took place, the early church became the church of the elite, and cultural and class differences took a toll on congregational diversity. A crucial task confronts us now: reviving the model of the early church and opening the doors of the church to all.

Congregations today can be diverse, too. In fact, the authors of *United by Faith* suggest that our congregations must be racially and culturally diverse in order to be faithful. In their opening argument they declare, "The explosion of racial and ethnic diversity in the United States has introduced dramatic tensions within faith communities. How should they respond to a pluralistic society?" Their answer: "The twenty-first must be the century of multiracial, multicultural congregations."[2]

We believe *we* are the ones we've been waiting for to make it happen. We can dismantle and "re-story" the prejudices and unconscious biases that segregate our houses of worship and become communities of hope and reconciliation. We come to this task with our own particular stories, having traveled on our own respective journeys of risking and learning, dealing with challenges and celebrating victories. Along the way, we have both ridden the roller coaster of highs and lows and discovered the joys and complexities of ministry in diverse settings.

Jacqui's story includes starting a new congregation in an urban setting that was intentionally multiracial and multicultural from its beginning; studying diverse congregations as the focus for her PhD dissertation; and serving the remarkably diverse congregation of Middle Collegiate Church in New York City for the past fourteen years. John's story includes serving a white congregation in an unusually diverse, culturally transitional urban neighborhood that had waited too long to adjust to demographic change; serving as senior interim minister in a large multicultural, multiracial congregation; and consulting with congregations to create strategies to expand their outreach to become more welcoming and diverse faith communities.

There is no way to sugarcoat it: this is challenging work. Creating authentically welcoming and inclusive faith communities that offer safe and brave space for all; helping people hear one another across borders of ethnicity and culture; and building trust and setting norms for sharing power and influence is hard work. Though the work is difficult, this is some of the most deeply rewarding work in ministry that we have ever experienced. The payoff? Offering God's people the opportunity to build communities that dismantle racism and xenophobia as we model the radical love of Christ to a broken world.

And this is urgent work. Unless we can finally come to terms with the brokenness of racism and effectively navigate cultural difference in this society, we will continue to be a nation divided against itself, with no end in sight. Can the church become a real force for healing? Will the church muster the courage to bring people together across ethnic, class, and cultural difference, congregation by congregation, and model the good community both in the sanctuary and the public square? We think it can. We have seen it work, and we have seen the energy, hope, and spirit that are released when it happens.

In this book we will explore how this transformation can happen and ten strategies that are essential for this journey, beginning with the call and commitment we believe is issued to all of the church as an urgent mandate to do this work.

Why the Pentecost Paradigm?

The miracle of Pentecost is that, somehow, people heard the stories of the good news of God's power on the earth in ways they could understand. Those Aramaic-speaking disciples preached the good news through their personalities to the personalities of those who were gathered. The reason the gospel caught fire is because those souls were eager for a story that fit, told in a way they could understand it. It was a story that made sense, one that gave their lives meaning and purpose. The gospel landed on them, meeting them where they were, and then lit them on fire with a vision of God's dream. The church was born in a cacophony of racial/ethnic and cultural diversity. Our churches simply have to be this way, too, in order to thrive in a rapidly changing world. The Spirit at work to call us to these communities of faith is what we mean by the *Pentecost Paradigm*!

Here are what we consider to be stages of congregational development toward the multiracial, multicultural future about which we both dream. These stages are not linear: a congregation might repeat a stage more than once due to the dynamics of change. Do you recognize your congregation in these descriptions? Determining your current stage will help you see what comes next and what steps will help your church move forward on its journey toward the love revolution needed to heal our souls and heal our nation of the scars of racism.

Stage 1: Awareness and a Growing Sense of Call

- Something happens. There is a racial or cultural shift in the community or an event on the national stage that calls attention to race and culture as issues with which to wrestle. This event might be a shift in school enrollment or a change in the "color" of the neighborhood. Perhaps there is a rash of violent events toward Muslims or people of color. There is a

growing sense of either opportunity or threat in the congregation. Even leaders who have been in denial about the changes awaken to a sense of calling and commitment.
- Leaders openly discuss possibilities and implications for ministry, within their congregation and with stakeholders in their communities. These stakeholders might include educators, service providers, or other clergy.
- Leaders might invite outside expertise to assist in assessment, readiness, and capacity building.
- A call and vision is articulated to the congregation, and a decision is made to proceed.

Stage 2: Steps toward Readiness

- Using the *Force Field Analysis* and *A Process for Visioning*, leaders articulate vision and goals and test feasibility.
- Congregants are invited to tell their stories in structured conversations; this begins to excavate formative attitudes on race and culture. This can be a programmatic focus in Black History Month, Asian History Month, or Hispanic American Heritage Month.
- Leaders and congregants read articles and books, like Ta'Nahesi Coates' *Between the World and Me*,[3] that open hearts and minds to the realities of racism. They discuss them in small groups.
- Structured conversations about the congregation's identity are happening.
- Staff and laity create new experiences in adult education and retreat settings, using films like *Crash* as a way to deepen conversations about race and culture.[4]
- Worship is planned to include guest preachers, choirs, and musicians of different cultures and ethnicities.
- Continuing education for clergy and staff focus on leading in multiracial, multicultural settings. Leaders work with a coach or spiritual mentor of a culture or ethnicity different from their own.
- Using resources like *Race: The Power of an Illusion* at PBS.org, leaders openly discuss the dynamics of *white privilege* and the power dynamics at work in diverse congregations. A culture of welcome is taking root among the leaders of the congregation.

Stage 3: Leading for Strategic Change

- Worship is routinely fashioned to educate, celebrate, and *story* the racial/ethnic and cultural diversity in God's creation. A wide range of musical genres is introduced, and worship becomes a celebration. Church school curriculum includes images and stories that encourage appreciation for diversity. There is intention about welcoming people of color to worship, and they are beginning to come.
- The congregation addresses racial and economic justice issues based on Scripture and its own vision and identity.
- Partnerships are formed with others in order to address concerns for the common good of the community.
- As efforts are initiated to reach new constituents, current members are held with care and compassion. Some signs of congregational discomfort are noticed.
- Greeters and ushers are trained in hospitality and cultural competencies.
- A Healing Racism Task Force is formed to study race more deeply and recommend strategies to leadership about changing congregational culture.

- Congregational identity begins to change, and a new identity emerges. The new identity of diversity and inclusion is reflected in the congregation, on the Web site, in social media, and in the public square.

Stage 4: Dealing with Disorientation or Disequilibrium

- Some members express discomfort with the changes occurring in the congregation; it is feared that those members might leave the church.
- More personal care and conversation are needed about what is changing and what is not.
- There are new expectations for clergy, staff, and lay leadership about how they prioritize their time.
- Laity are encouraged to rethink their role as leaders and refocus their energies; an attitude of experimentation is encouraged.
- Conflict may increase and will need to be addressed quickly. The vision for a diverse and inclusive faith community is continually rehearsed.

Stage 5: Achieving 20 Percent Nonmajority Critical Mass

- Multiple strategies are in place to tell the congregation's story to its members and to the larger community.
- Power sharing and leadership development are normative in the congregation. People of color are in key leadership roles, and cross-racial, cross-cultural relationships are well established. New members of color share their stories, which are welcomed; they change the congregational story.
- Staff, lay leadership, organizational structure, and budget reflect new priorities.
- The congregation has become antiracist in its mission. Members participate in addressing issues of common concern in the community. They attend public meetings and have a working relationship with local government and the school system.
- The congregation has a public reputation for innovation and welcome. The congregation is seen as a brave and safe space in which all are welcomed. It is known as a place of convening for the larger community.

We hope you will use this book in conversation with other leaders in your context and consider it a roadmap to the future to which our God calls us. We can only build the reign of God on earth and break down the walls that divide us while being in community together across the human-made boundaries of race and ethnicity. Writing this book has been a challenging yet joyful undertaking. We welcome you to the conversation.

Chapter 1

Embracing Call and Commitment

*O*n April 16, 1963, in his *Letter from a Birmingham City Jail*, the Rev. Dr. Martin Luther King Jr. wrote, "I have almost reached the regrettable conclusion that the Negro's great stumbling block in the stride toward freedom is not the White Citizen's Councilor or the Ku Klux Klanner, but the white moderate who is more devoted to "order" than to justice."[1]

We are issuing a particular call to the white church. During the Civil Rights Movement of the 1950s and 1960s, numerous black clergy, including Dr. King, appealed to the white church for support and active engagement. The movement hoped for financial, political, and moral support from the white church. Much of the white church responded with either silence or outright disdain that King and other civil rights leaders were threatening the status quo. This is not to ignore the courageous engagement by some whites who marched, sat-in, and spoke out publicly for the cause. Some white clergy, moved by the call to prophetic involvement, paid the ultimate price, losing their lives at the hands of white supremacists. Others lost their livelihoods when their congregations took opposing positions and fired their minister for involvement in the cause for civil rights.

Much of the white church, however, hunkered down in fear and anger, disoriented by the social upheaval challenging the assumptions of white privilege. Reading the climate in their congregations, many clergy chose to steer clear of a prophetic role in favor of maintaining a comfortable relationship with their congregations.

And where is the white church now? Many churches have abandoned addressing controversial social justice issues altogether in the cause of congregational peace, leaving the work to advocacy groups and the legal system. Many congregations have focused on noncontroversial mission endeavors that tend to be at some geographical distance from them and have avoided lending their voices and presence to the hard stuff of economic injustice, Black Lives Matter, and confronting hate speech and anti-immigrant rhetoric. Too many white churches busy themselves with activities that include raising money to fight malaria in Africa or volunteering with Habitat for Humanity, all good causes but far too safe for the needed social change on the high-stakes issues at our doorstep.

Many whites occupying the pews in worship on Sunday mornings take issue with the phrase "Black Lives Matter," insisting that "all lives matter," and accusing the Black Lives Matter movement of being racist itself. Such arguments and attitudes constitute a fault line that has run deeply in our American culture, stretching back to this nation's founding and laying bare this manifestation of racial bigotry. This is an example of white denial and, often enough, an intentional strategy to suppress and camouflage the realities of race-based injustice that permeate our society. Accusing the victims of racism of being racist themselves for calling attention to the blatant discrimination in our nation reveals the desperation found in a transparent lie. For these white accusers, "black lives matter" implies that white lives somehow are diminished in value when black lives matter at least as much as white lives. The historical proposition that white lives are intrinsically superior to black lives is at play here. But insisting that all lives matter dilutes the claim that black lives matter even in the current context of a rash of hate crimes and police killings of unarmed African Americans. The reality is that all lives will matter only when black lives matter, native peoples' lives matter, immigrants' lives matter, and LGBTQ lives matter. When all are as free from bias, violence, and discrimination as are the majority of white people, *then* it can be said that all lives matter.

A Call to All Congregations

We believe God calls all of the church to the work of inclusion, justice, and peacemaking. And we believe that every monocultural congregation is called to dismantle racism and xenophobia. That means embracing the diversity in our communities and leading the larger culture on issues of inclusion. These might be challenging words for some African American congregations that were historically forced out of white churches to become exclusively monocultural congregations of color. Such congregations became and still serve as islands of safety and cultural survival in a sea of hostility. But the one we follow into mission and ministry—Jesus the Christ—was an avowed boundary crosser, a reformer of the religious and secular culture of his time. We are in good company when we lead the way on radical inclusion of those different from ourselves. In some contexts that might mean a black church reaching out to Korean neighbors, a Latino congregation starting a ministry to immigrant families from North Africa, or a Chinese church hosting an afterschool program for African American junior high students. It will also require that all of us be open to shifting our worship culture to include a wider range of music, multiple voices in leadership, and incorporating spiritual practices valued in other cultural settings. We believe the commitment to inclusion and diversity is a high calling, issued to all who count themselves as Christians, no matter what our ethnicity or culture.

When we accept the notion that God is not ambivalent about any of this; when we acknowledge that the Hebrew and Christian Scriptures repeatedly advocate for those left out, the stranger, the poor and oppressed, only then will we be able to draw on our faith tradition as a resource for truth telling that contributes to national healing.

God has not called the church to circle the wagons in the interest of the status quo or avoid issues that challenge dominant thought; nor has God called the church into community for comfort alone. It is the faith community that must question conventional wisdom. The church is uniquely called to confront injustice, exclusion, and fear. The truth is that much of the church has not done the work it needs to do on issues of race, class, sexual orientation, and gender. It is also true that much of the church has too often avoided difficult conversations in the interest of congregational harmony. In so doing, congregations create a culture of silence on these issues. Rather than create discomfort, congregations have accepted the false social construct of "race" and embraced an underdeveloped theology that reinforces the siloing of human community into separateness. Addressing racism and xenophobia should be viewed by faith communities as an essential spiritual practice.

Except for 8 to 10 percent of Protestant churches, congregations continue to be as racially segregated and exclusive as they were reaching back to this nation's founding. In this regard, much of the larger culture is moving beyond these outdated constructs, sometimes at break-neck speed, leaving the church in the dust of its settled ways. Any congregation—white, black, or otherwise—that is "more devoted to order than to justice"[2] and disengaged from "breaking down the dividing walls of hostility" (cf. Ephesians 2:14) has lost its way.

While much has changed since the Civil Rights Movement of the 1950s and 1960s, much has not. In fact, it can be argued that ground has been lost in the fight for justice and equality. Voter suppression, the gerrymandering of voting districts, school resegregation, the school-to-prison pipeline, and the broad-brush demonization of immigrants, refugees, and non-Christian populations are battle lines in the fight for justice and equality. Addressing the potentially controversial issues of race, class, gender, national origin, and religious practice is urgent work.

This book is a call to the noninvolved, play-it-safe church to engage in its own work of education, dialogue, advocacy, and action to set right the divisions cutting across this country. It is also a call to every congregation to work for inclusion and equality; to respect and value the uniqueness of every person and culture; and to commit to reaching across the dividing lines separating us all into groups based on the color of our skin, the accents in our speech, and our national origins. In our current political climate, there is a real threat of being dragged backward from our vision of a just, free, and inclusive society. The church must have a voice that advocates for justice, equality, and inclusion. Prayer will not be nearly enough.

Since the Civil Rights Movement, we have seen legislation passed and subverted, progress made and reversed. We have seen the "Stop-and-Frisk" and "Stand Your Ground" policies take their toll on people of color. We have awakened to the prejudicial application of drug laws resulting in far higher incarceration rates for people of color than whites for the same offense, and we have had the curtain pulled back on the school-to-prison pipeline.

If we ever questioned the depth of division in this country, we need do so no longer. The nation's demographic shift and accompanying backlash coupled with economic anxiety among lower-class and middle-class whites has fomented what can be argued as a crisis in race relations, class, and cultural differences. Some feel that white supremacy is now on full display in many parts of the country. There is a rise in hate speech and hate crimes against Muslims, Mexicans, Jews, and the LGBTQ community. A culture of violence against minorities, especially against people of color, has become normative in the minds of many, as unprovoked police shootings of unarmed African Americans has led the news cycle on too many days alongside the hate-filled, sickening attacks on police officers.

There is strong evidence that, as we have neared the tipping point toward becoming a society with no ethnic majority, we see a rising up of political populism, a call for the abandonment of "political correctness," and a crisis of national identity based on race and xenophobia. Some are asking, "Who are we if we are not a predominantly white, Christian nation free of the burden of having to navigate the complexities of diversity and justice for all?" These issues are now haunting our nation and challenging our faith communities.

Christian faith communities must also come to terms with their own identity issues and address some challenging questions of their own. Often these are not new questions, but they spring from the very founding of the faith itself. The church has always had to contend with the values of the secular order in the face of the claims of the gospel. We are living in a time of deep ferment; a time of profound injustices and inequities; and sadly, a time when the voice of many faith communities is muted, mired in ambivalence, and stuck in long-standing patterns of avoidance, fear, and confusion. Needed now are our persistent soul-searching and our outcry over the immorality of economic disparity, racial injustice, and white privilege. Urgently needed now are our presence and our voice in the public square and our commitment to see past the subterfuges of the powerful. Ever wooed by the conveniences and contrivances of the dominant culture, the faith community is easily distracted and quickly diluted. It is the church's role to rehearse the promise and hope at the center of the faith community's identity and simultaneously challenge the values and injustices of the dominant culture.

Further, it is necessary to distinguish between the calls for patriotism and the claims of the faith tradition if the church is to fulfill its role in the larger society. The values of the secular order and the values of the faith tradition are often conflated, with religion being coopted in the service of personal and national agendas. Examples of this are found on public display from appeals to God during State of the Union speeches to prayers before football games to the American flag prominently located in the sanctuaries of houses of worship. Allegiance to God and country are not interchangeable nor of comparable value. The prophetic task is to critique the secular order rather than be held captive by it. Therefore, we look upon the conduct of government with suspicion and through the lens of the sacred texts and the faith traditions. Given the tensions in our nation and in much of the church, it is urgent that we clarify our moral center as a people and declare our call to seek the common good on behalf of the human community. Without a deep sense of call and a tenacious commitment to this work; without the resolve to explore our own journey and our spiritual interior; without a willingness to excavate our own prejudices, motives, and biases, we will not be ready to exert spiritual leadership in this work of healing.

Our Calling to Spiritual Leadership

Ministry has often been defined as categorically different from occupational choice or even vocational pursuit. Rooted not in cultural expectations for productivity, but in ancient religious story and metaphor, ministry is entered into as a "calling." This calling is born of the tradition of priest and prophet, of one chosen to speak for God, to protect and administer the moral code of personal and corporate conduct, to define the believer's relationship to the Holy, and to articulate revealed truth as a way to advance human community. We experience this calling so profoundly that we have no choice but to say "yes" to it even when we feel inadequate to the task; even when doing so could jeopardize our security, our peace of mind, and our physical comfort.

In the broadest terms, our call embraces advocating for those on the margins, the poor, the vulnerable, and those treated unjustly. Captured in biblical texts and story is the mandate to address issues of injustice and oppression, to seek the common good, to seek to bring into harmony all that is broken and at odds with God's vision for human community. Division based on race and culture can only be worked out in diverse community. There is an urgent need to come together and not be driven farther apart by the divisions in the larger culture.

The act of committing to this calling and being claimed by it brings us to experience the utter defeat of personal agendas and private aspirations. Our response to this sense of call results in making commitments capable of depleting the very soul that yesterday it caused to soar. To honor this calling is to be alternately stretched and blessed, affirmed and challenged, nurtured by renewing waters, and driven into the desert. It is to live with absolute certainty one moment and complete vulnerability the next. It is to identify oneself with the greatest of all hopes in the face of the greatest of all possible disillusionments. Living out this calling means journeying on the coattails of a promise as elusive as the evening mist.

A calling to spiritual leadership also requires tending to one's own inner life, exploring fearlessly what Parker Palmer calls the "shadow" side of ourselves, and bringing to the surface our inner life as the path to spiritual depth. Understanding how our inner life shapes our public role and possessing the self-awareness to understand the inner forces that motivate and constrain us—these skills form a vital leadership capacity. Being connected to the deeper places within us opens the possibility for congruence and authenticity in our relationships and in our role as spiritual leaders. In *Let Your Life Speak*, Palmer states, "A *good* leader is intensely aware of the interplay of inner shadow and light, lest the act of leadership do more harm than good."[3] This self-knowledge is the greatest safeguard against posing behind the many masks we are tempted to wear. It allows for maintaining a proper balance between vulnerability and control and fends off self-deception. This is true for individual leaders and true for congregations as well. It is especially true in multiracial, multicultural ministry settings where diversity and inclusion create complex dynamics not experienced in monocultural ministry settings. I (Jacqui) am so convinced of the importance of self-knowledge that I require all of my clergy staff to be in a relationship with a coach, spiritual director, or therapist to process the complexities and emotional content of this work. In order to be an effective leader in these settings, a high level of emotional intelligence is needed.

It is our experience that in multiracial, multicultural settings, communication is often burdened not only by our personal stories but also by the stories of our ancestors. When we try to wade into the deeper waters of self-revelation, when we share our stories of who we are, we find that these cross-racial and cross-cultural engagements are often cautious and hesitating. We quickly become aware of our limits to tell each other our truths, to explore our complex feelings and attitudes regarding the ways in which race has impacted and even shaped us. Will there be questions about our intentions? Will we be accused of "playing the race card" or being blind to our own racism or unconscious bias?

A calling to lead in multiracial, multicultural ministry settings means constantly and affirmatively articulating the value, the vision, and the counter-cultural nature of these diverse faith communities. This is especially important amid the rise of white supremacy and the normalization of bias for cultural exclusion, isolation, and racial segregation. It is the task of spiritual leadership to step out and announce the dream of a healed and reconciled world and to confront the dream stealers who are content with the status quo, where the identity of too many faith communities is determined by skin color and where eleven o'clock on Sunday morning is still the most segregated hour in our society.

Our Prophetic Role

Multiracial, multicultural faith communities also have a unique prophetic role in the larger society. In his book *The Prophetic Imagination*, Walter Brueggemann states, "The task of prophetic ministry is to nurture, nourish, and evoke a consciousness and perception alternative to the consciousness and perception of the dominant culture around us."[4] It is out of this alternative consciousness that the faith community finds its identity and defines its purpose.

In this sense and in every respect, the faith community is subversive in its relationship to the dominant culture and is not beguiled by the culture's claims of affinity with the faith community, illustrated by the words "In God We Trust" printed on the coin of the realm.

Against these challenges, the prophetic function must rely on a deep sense of tradition and history. The faith community must find its story in God's story and rehearse God's consistent faithfulness in the midst of the people's despair. In doing so it uses what Brueggemann calls "the language of hope" and "the language of amazement," which reestablishes God's radical vision of a new social reality.[5]

The prophetic role finds expression when the faith community engages the larger culture on matters that concern the common good and when it lifts up the vision of a new social reality. In preforming the prophetic role, it is not enough that the faith community addresses only itself, its beliefs, and its behavior. The larger culture must also hear the word of the Lord. In his book *Doing Justice*, Dennis Jacobsen observes, "The church enters the public arena in order to be the church, in order to be true to itself, in order to be faithful to its Lord, in order to heed the summons of the Holy Spirit."[6] Engaging in public ministry means entering the public square and addressing the moral and social issues affecting the local, national, and global community. It means making common cause with partners who also have a vision for healing and wholeness in the larger context. It means assuming the role of public advocate, creating dialogue that is public and inclusive, and representing an alternative vision to that of dominant culture. We are propelled into the public arena because God is there, because our faith is not compartmentalized and does not confine itself to the sanctuary.

Making a Personal Commitment

Monoracial, monoethnic, and monocultural faith communities exist for many reasons. They have helped generations of immigrants, First Nations people, and formerly enslaved African people feel safe as they navigate a predominately white, English-speaking nation and a culture often experienced as hostile to them. These faith communities have served to mitigate language barriers and provide a familiar context for those marginalized by the larger culture. Sadly, the history of slavery and the reality of racism in the United States of America is the fundamental reason our congregations are so often segregated.

Even so, the vision for racially, ethnically, and culturally diverse congregations has its roots in the promise of God's shalom, in a healed world—*tikkun olam* in Hebrew. The story of a healed world is articulated in the sacred texts of many faith traditions. Islam, Hinduism, Buddhism, Christianity, and Judaism all have texts that envision healed bodies, minds, and spirits. It is our personal commitment to a healed world that will lead to the dismantling of racism, heterosexism, and classism in our nation. In order to heal the world, we have to commit to changing the current story.

As a child, growing up in a working-class neighborhood in the Philadelphia suburbs, I (John) lived most of my young life in the bubble of "whiteness." I had virtually no awareness of issues of race or class, with the exception of my father's occasional bigoted and racist invectives. It wasn't until the early 1960s that I became conscious of the racial turmoil in the country as I watched the evening news and saw film footage of peaceful protesters being beaten and set upon by police dogs. At that moment in time the relatively new technology of television was the instrument through which I was educated about race, and today it is the cell phone video. I can't explain exactly why, but the scenes on the television aroused in me a deep sense of outrage and injustice.

Prior to that, there were the stories told to me by my mother about my grandfather. As a young man, he opened a corner store and butcher shop. I have the photograph of that store, showing my grandfather behind the counter. This photograph was probably taken around 1930. As the story goes, his customers included both black and white residents in the community. To my grandmother's chagrin, my grandfather was known to "carry some families on the books," meaning that he allowed them to buy food they could not then pay for on the promise they would pay when they could. Some of those families were black folks. It wasn't long before the local chapter of the Klan learned how he was accommodating these black families and organized a boycott of the store, driving my grandfather out of business. This took place in Philadelphia, the city of brotherly love. My grandparents' experience stands as a marker for me in my growing awareness of race in this country and its manifestation in the story of my own family.

At the age of sixteen, after experiencing a call to ministry and receiving the support of my congregation, my pastor asked me to preach one Sunday morning. I knew very little of the Bible then, and so I selected the text most familiar to me, the story of the Good Samaritan. In the sermon, which I was asked to write on my own, I referenced Dr. Martin Luther King Jr. as an example of the Good Samaritan. Following worship the chair of the board of trustees of the church lingered behind to speak to me. He laid into me for comparing King to the Good Samaritan, declaring that "that man is a Communist" and troublemaker and not someone who should even be mentioned in a sermon. This was my first experience of "not being white enough," a concept explored in *Learning to Be White*, by Thandeka.[7] When one is not white enough, she argues, one has chosen to identify with the "other" in addition to aligning oneself with one's own ethnic heritage. When one is not white enough, one risks surrendering the shelter of the white community and the assurance of the privileges that go with being white. Of course, I could not have articulated this at that young age, but the message that I had stepped outside the bounds of my white identity was clear. I would also learn later that for a black person, there was such a thing as not being black enough, not behaving in accord with the cultural signatures of "blackness," and thereby being ostracized by some in the black community. Tennis player Arthur Ashe wrote poignantly about this. Remnants of these dynamics still manifest for Jacqui and me in reactions to our interracial marriage.

My college years in Appalachia were an education in poverty when, as a student, I served small congregations in towns and rural settlements in the hills and hollers of Eastern Kentucky. The aching deprivation of this poverty suffered by whites and blacks later helped me understand the racial chasm between them that dominated their otherwise common lot. It was a chasm engineered by the white plantation elite at the founding of the nation, to divide this potential alliance and prevent it from joining forces against the white power structure.

In summary, then, we argue that the church is called to multiracial, multicultural community life. The vision for this call is manifest in our Scriptures. We are urging leaders to make a personal commitment to this urgent work and to network with and learn from others on this journey.

Throughout this book are exercises designed to help you (as an individual reader or, ideally, as part of a leadership team studying this book together) explore and vision together how to grow and develop a more multiracial, multicultural congregation. This first exercise (below) is intended to set a context for assessing where your congregation is on the journey toward greater diversity and inclusion.

෬෬෬෬෬෬

Review Stage 1 of the Pentecost Paradigm

– Can you identify with this profile (described on p. 3)?

_____

_____

_____

_____

_____

_____

_____

_____

_____

– What is your personal story, and how has it prepared you for this work?

_____

_____

_____

_____

_____

_____

_____

_____

SELF-ASSESSMENT QUESTIONS

Questions of Call

   1. How would you describe your sense of call to this multiracial, multicultural work?

   2. How have you honored this call during the past year?

   3. What have been the constraints to living out this calling?

   4. If you were to live out this calling more faithfully, what would you add to your ministry? What would be deleted?

Questions of Self-Knowledge

   1. What are your unspoken hopes and constraining fears imagining your congregation becoming more racially, culturally diverse?

   2. What are the steps you might take to assist the congregation to become more diverse?

   3. As a leader, in what ways do you avoid difficult issues? What is going on inside you when this happens?

Questions of Prophetic Role

1. How do you understand your prophetic role? How does this role find expression in your work and the congregation's ministry?

2. What are the risks God may be inviting you to take now?

3. What is your vision for a new social order? How do you promote it?

4. How have you and the congregation given leadership to the larger community in the interest of racial justice?

Chapter 2

Casting the Vision

Vision Is Personal

It was 2003, and I (Jacqui) was completing my PhD at Drew University while working as a Senior Consultant at the Alban Institute. In the one place, I was doing an academic study of leaders in multiracial, multicultural congregations. In the other, I was heading a project called Negotiating Cultural Boundaries, consulting on race and culture in congregations, denominational systems, and for the U.S. Navy. More than anything, I was living out a vision that had been planted in my soul as a child.

I was raised by parents who had seen and experienced the harshness of racial segregation in the Jim Crow South. Mom was raised in Ruleville, Mississippi, with her sister and brother. Their mother, our "Ma Dear," was abandoned by their father, who moved north in the Great Migration. She worked as a nursing assistant and sharecropped a piece of land, raising her children all by herself. Mom sang in the choir with social justice activist Fannie Lou Hamer; Hamer's close friend, Uncle George, helped register people to vote in the Freedom Summer of 1964. Dad grew up in Meridian, Mississippi, not too far from where the bodies of Chaney, Goodman, and Schwerner were found that summer of 1964. Like Mom, Dad walked past the "School" to attend the "Colored School" on the edge of town. His mother fought off white men who wanted to take her land. Dad escaped Jim Crow by joining the Air Force. He and Mom met on a base in Lincoln, Nebraska, where they fell in love, got married, and had me. Their intention was to raise black children who were not hobbled by the burden of racism in our nation, not if they could help it.

I was five years old and in kindergarten when we settled in Portsmouth, New Hampshire, and I learned my first race lesson. I was close friends with two little boys, both named Tommy, one blond and the other a redhead, until a little girl named Lisa moved to town. She brought attitudes she had learned from adults in Mississippi to my happy, well-adjusted little New Hampshire Air Force Base world, viewpoints that shattered my sense of safety. She told me and the two Tommies that I was a "dirty n-word," and that I got "chocolate milk" from my mother's breasts. I don't know where it came from, certainly not from my parents, but I hurled a singsongy little ditty at her in which I called her a "cracker"!

When I told my parents about her behavior and mine, they scolded me, saying all people are beloved of God, and name-calling was not acceptable. My dad went to the base supervisor and lodged a complaint about Lisa and her parents, and my mom had one of those talks that black parents have with their children. "Baby, this sounds really silly, but believe it or not, some people might not like you just because you are black. But you are a Lewis. God loves you, we love you, and you can do anything you want to do, be anything you want to be, if you work hard."

That night, along with my "Now I lay me down to sleep" ritual prayer, I remember praying, "God, please make it be so that no matter what their skin color, everyone will be loved."

Though they were raised in the harshest, most racist conditions, my parents had inherited from their ancestors and from their church a vision of a healed and whole world, one in which all people were seen as equal and everyone would have enough. They bequeathed that vision to me, and I took it deeply into my soul. Though I had not yet heard the "I have a dream" speech of the Rev. Dr. Martin Luther King Jr., I was praying his dream that folk would be judged not by the color of their skin but by the content of their character.

Over time I came to see how that episode with Lisa shaped my call to ministry, my commitment to a world freed of racism, and the vision that would guide my life and work. As a student of the Bible, I am inspired by the articulation of this vision in Zechariah—a dream of a time when old people will sit in the city streets, watching children safely playing (Zechariah 8). It is also rooted in Revelation, and the picture of the renewed holy city, with a river running through it. There are trees on either side of the river, and on each of those trees are leaves for the healing of all the nations, all the people (Revelation 21–22). All the people, of many tribes and places, praise God in one voice (Revelation 7).

My commitment to and vision for racial healing was cemented further when my hero was assassinated while working for racial and economic equality. As bullets flew by our windows in our South Side Chicago home, and I hid under my bed with my sister, I felt a call in my soul to pick up the mantle of the Rev. Dr. Martin Luther King Jr. to also be what he called "a drum major for justice" and to march with God's people toward liberation. My parents' stories, my own story, and the salvific story of God's commitment to heal our souls and heal the world have caused me to see a world free of racism, and to imagine my role in creating that. This vision has caused me to be a bridge-builder, a boundary crosser, a truth teller, a strategist, and a reconciler—all of these as roles to help dismantle the racism and delusions of white supremacy that shape policies, laws, and systems in our nation.

I love this text from Isaiah: "I am about to do a new thing; now it springs forth, do you not perceive it? I will make a way in the wilderness and rivers in the desert" (Isaiah 43:19).

In order to see what God is up to, in order to perceive God's vision, we must not only exegete the Scriptures to find God's call and plan; we must also exegete our own stories, examining them for vivid glimpses of holy imagination and also for blind spots that might hinder our ability to see what God sees for us.

What is your story? Use the following exercise for some personal reflection on your own story that will help set the stage for deep vision conversations with your team.

WHAT IS YOUR STORY?

An Exercise in Exegeting the Self

1. Recall the first time you were "othered" or rejected for being you. What happened?

2. What did your family of origin teach you about race/ethnicity?

3. What did your family of origin teach you about gender and sexuality?

4. How has your understanding of racial/ethnic identity changed over time? How has it remained the same?

5. How has your understanding of sexuality and gender changed over time? How has it remained the same?

6. Talk about "class" in your story. Where have you been "othered" or othered another because of class differences?

7. When did you first other another for their race/ethnicity, gender, or sexuality?

8. Is there something that needs to be confessed, forgiven, or changed around race, ethnicity, or class in your life?

9. Is there something that needs to be confessed, forgiven, or changed around gender and sexuality in your life?

10. If life in your faith community is an ongoing story, what is the title of the current chapter? What is the title five years from now? Write the title of three episodes that must happen in order to change the story.

Vision Is Communal

The writer of Proverbs reminds us that without a vision people perish. As a congregational leader, whether lay or clergy, old or young, part of our responsibility is to see for ourselves and to help others see what God is up to in the world. In other words, we are theologians in residence in our contexts, helping our communities to become part of God's vision, to find their role in the story God is writing with us. Of course, what we see, how we see it, and how we interpret what we see in our community is theological work, shaped in and through our own stories. One clear source for theological visioning is our Scriptures.

In order to grow multiracial, multicultural congregations, we must look at Scripture through the lens of liberation: in our own stories and in the stories of our community, we remember the liberating work of God. The God of exodus, the God of sight giving and healing is the God who calls us to communities of radical love and inclusion. This is the God who indeed has made all humans of equal worth and in God's image (Genesis 1 and 2; Psalm 139). This God breaks the chains of white supremacy, racism, and xenophobia. This God heals us of the fear that difference can cause in us and instead encourages us not only to accept difference but also to embrace and celebrate it.

The story of God in the world has a beginning, a middle, and an end. In the beginning, the Hebrew Scriptures declare, is God. First a Spirit is hovering over the deep. Then a voice is calling the creation into being. Partnering with the Human One. Offering guidance in Wisdom, Law, and Prophets. The Word made flesh, and the flesh made word, living among us. The very reign of God itself, within us, among us, and storied in parables, preaching, and teaching. Love that will not die, that outlives death. Love that meets its followers in Jerusalem. The Spirit descending such that all the gathered people hear the good news in their own language. A firestorm of Holy Spirit action spreading the good news in the known, radically diverse world.

This story is our story; we are the called-out ones, beautiful in our diversity, created in the image of the one who calls us into being. Created out of love, for love, designed to be partners, to be reconciled to the Creator, to one another, and to all of creation. This creation, Paul says, is waiting like a woman groaning in childbirth, eager for the children of God to show themselves (Rom. 8:22–25). And show ourselves we must. As whole, healed, repaired, reconciled, complete because we exist together, splendid and delightful in a pantone of shades of white, beige, brown, and black. No longer conscribed by the gender binary of male and female, we sometimes defy category: we as a people show ourselves to be male, female, transgender, and two-spirit people. We are same-gender loving, straight, and bisexual. We are, by design, reverently and wonderfully made!

Vision Is Strategic

Vision helps us to see the world through God's eyes, to see the world as it can be. A vision by definition critiques the status quo. It is lofty, inviting, and aspirational: it organizes the work of our systems and congregations. It defines priorities and determines how resources—money, people, and time—are to be allocated. The vision becomes the "boss" or the steward of the shared life of the community. The vision sets priorities, defines goals, and draws people to a picture of a preferred reality. A vision is best developed through conversation, meditation, and prayer rather than by someone who declares the vision "from on high" and announces it from a position of power. Because a clear and compelling vision delineates what the community will and will not do, it is vital that the community "owns" the vision and actively participates in its articulation.

When I came to Middle Collegiate Church in January 2004, the consistory (our board) had been searching for a new Senior Minister and had done really important work on identity and vision. They had asked, "What is the *essential Middle Church*?" They understood that the essential Middle had something to do with who their longtime pastor Gordon Dragt was and with his radically welcoming personality. They also knew that it had something to do with who Middle Church is at the core: its history, values, and *Sitz im Leben* (situation in life). During the 1980s, when thousands of people were dying of AIDS in the East Village of Manhattan, Middle Church was the safe place to gather for funerals. On September 11, 2001, Middle Church was the safe place for people making their way north from Ground Zero, covered in ash and tears. Radical welcome and justice works are in our DNA. Through one-to-one conversations and in focus groups guided by prayer, our leaders listened for the hopes, dreams, and the call of our congregation. When they pondered what Middle Church would look like in five years, the consistory adopted this vision statement in March 2005:

> Middle Collegiate Church is a celebrating, culturally diverse, inclusive and growing community of faith where all persons are welcomed just as they are as they come through the door. Rooted in Christian tradition as the oldest continuous Protestant Church in North America, Middle Church is called by God to boldly do a new thing on the earth.
> As a teaching congregation that celebrates the arts, our ministries include rich and meaningful worship, care and education that nurture the mind, body, and spirit, social action which embraces the global community, and participation in interfaith dialogue for the purpose of justice and reconciliation.

Where a mission statement might be more generic ("Go and make disciples of all the nations," for example), a vision statement is specific, about a particular time and place. It answers the question, "If we do what we are called to do, what will our congregation and community look like and be like at a specific time, in three years or five years from now?"

Asking this question anew, with our congregation outgrowing our space, and rethinking how we will use staff and laity to do our work, here is the first draft of a "Vision 2020" statement our staff and board have gleaned from conversation and prayer. It is, today, a work in progress, but I like where it is going. I think it will take us to 2020 and beyond.

> Middle Collegiate Church is a multicultural, multiethnic, intergenerational movement of Spirit and justice, powered by Revolutionary Love, with room for all. Following in the Way of Jesus' radical love, and inspired by the prophets, **Middle Church is called by God to do a bold new thing on the earth.** We aim to heal the soul and the world by dismantling racist, classist, sexist, and homophobic systems of oppression. Because our God is still speaking in many languages, we work in inter-religious partnerships to uproot injustice, eradicate poverty, care for the brokenhearted, and build the Reign of God on earth. This activism is fueled by our faith; our faith is expressed in art; our art is an active prayer connecting us with the Holy Spirit. Founded prior to this nation, Middle Church affirms the transformative power of moral imagination, reclaiming and reframing Christianity inside our walls, on the street, and in virtual spaces around the globe.

Even though times have changed and even though our vision statement has changed, we remain clear that we are called to do a bold new thing on the earth and that all people—no matter their race/ethnicity, gender/gender performance, sexual orientation, age, or position in life—are awesomely and wonderfully made in the image of God. We believe God is indeed doing a new thing (Isa. 43:19) in and through us. Therefore, we decided to repeat this phrase in our new vision statement. This statement says something about not only our vision, but also our ongoing sense of identity.

Some texts that might be helpful to you in your vision process include Lovett Weems's *Church Leadership: Vision, Team, Culture, Integrity,*[1] Gil Rendle and Alice Mann's *Holy Conversations: Strategic Planning as a Spiritual Practice for Congregations,*[2] and Jacqueline J. Lewis's book *The Power of Stories: A Guide for Leading Multiracial and Multicultural Congregations.*[3]

Discuss the Process for Visioning below (a tool we have used at Middle Church, inspired by conversations with many colleagues) to plan next steps for your congregation.

WRITING THE VISION AND MAKING IT PLAIN

A Process for Visioning

1. *Commission a Vision Team.* Invite three to four members of your board and members of the congregation for a total of eight to twelve team members. "Cast" diversity that represents the preferred future (age, gender/sexuality, race/ethnicity, vocation, economic situation). If you are reading this book as part of an already-established Vision Team, move on to Step 2!

2. *Meet to deploy tasks.* The Vision Team will use surveys and structured conversations with individuals and focus groups to gather hopes and dreams, review the data, and draft a vision statement and ministry plan, including goals and objectives.

3. *The Vision Team specifically gathers data* from
   - Focus groups—at church and house gatherings
   - Congregational meetings—twice a year
   - One-on-one conversations with key leaders, stakeholders, allies, and critics

4. *Concurrently, staff gathers data* from
   - One-on-one conversations with congregants and community members (local schools, social service agencies, mission partners)
   - Ministry by walking around (mapping the assets in the community with an eye toward what is already being offered in the community)
   - MissionInsite or Percept Demographics
   - Surveys in worship or with online tools like Survey Monkey

5. *Ask these questions* in your conversations with one another, staff, congregants, and community members:
   - If vision is the picture of a preferred reality, what do you see in five years? Be specific. What does the congregation look like? What are people doing? Learning? What kinds of relationships do they have? What does the community/neighborhood look like? What does the staff look like?

   - What three things do we need to do in order to get to the five-year vision?

— What one thing should we let go of in order to get there?

— In our congregation, we say we do _____ well, but we could do better.

6. As the Vision Team reviews the data from inside and outside, ask:
   — What new insights do we glean from this conversation?

   — What is one implication for our planning?

   — What is the story we hear about our congregation in the community?

   — What unique thing can we offer to the community in partnership?

   — The Vision Team presents a vision and plan to the board, which approves it. The board shares the plan with the congregation and celebrates it often.

In conclusion, the vision for multiracial, multicultural congregations is cast from many sources, among them our personal stories, the ongoing story of God's interaction with human-kind, and the circumstances in our current situation. We are given insight that is personal, communal, and strategic and called to respond to what we see. Seeing is the first step in part-nering with God to heal our souls and heal the world.

Review Stages 1 and 2 of the Pentecost Paradigm

– Are you ready to formulate a vision for growing a multiracial faith community?

_____

_____

_____

_____

_____

_____

– What concrete steps will you take first?

_____

_____

_____

_____

_____

– How are you generating support for this journey?

_____

_____

_____

_____

_____

Chapter 3

Managing Change and Resistance

*T*here is now a large body of research regarding the dynamics of change and resistance. This research confirms that even small changes in the life of institutions can be difficult to manage and will generate resistance. This resistance may be in the form of anger; passive-aggressive behaviors; grief due to a sense of loss, confusion, and malaise; or outright refusal to perform needed tasks. This research also notes that change is more challenging in complex systems. Congregations are complex human systems. Change and the accompanying resistance in complex human systems are influenced by context, values, beliefs, and norms.

A Case Study of Resistance

We have seen congregations in demographically changing communities deny or ignore these shifting realities at their own peril. Often ill equipped to imagine reaching out to new residents of a different culture or ethnicity, congregations simultaneously observe that their current members are growing older and the congregation is in decline. Even though reaching out to a demographically changing community is in the congregation's best interests, they may make the unspoken choice to remain as they are for as long as they can. They choose the past rather than the future. This was the circumstance when a new minister arrived to serve a congregation in a small city in New Jersey. The congregation had circled the wagons as the community around them went through a demographic transition from mostly white to mixed to mostly nonwhite. The congregation and the ministers of the previous fifteen or more years had colluded to keep silent about this as black, Hispanic, and Asian people moved into the community and their white neighbors moved out. This change reflected the classic pattern of white flight as home values declined, community services relocated, and congregations either moved out or withered in place but did nothing to address the concerns of the community around them or invite newcomers into the life of the church. When the new minister arrived, he urged the congregation's leadership to create a study group to explore options available to the congregation, though they were considerably behind the curve in their response to this demographic change.

The congregation was in a real bind. They resented the newcomers for the disruption "they" had caused and yet still hoped to rescue the value of their life's investment represented in the house they had worked many years to purchase, and in which they had raised their children. This white working-class congregation was stuck with their anger, grief, and confusion. These feelings were on full display when some neighborhood children, children of color known to the minister but not to the congregation, knocked on the minister's door one Halloween asking if they could come to the party the church was having. The minister naturally said "yes" and sent them across the street to the church, where the party was underway. Off they ran, full of excitement and bouncing with energy. In a matter of seconds, they were back at the minister's door to report that they were told the party was only for the children of the church. The minister then escorted them back across the street to the door of the church social hall, which was now locked. He knocked on the door and was met by a member of the church board, red-faced with anger, who launched into a hostile verbal lashing of the neighborhood children before she saw the minister standing there. "These children were not invited," the board member sputtered to the minister. In that instant it was clear that there was more work to be done here than there would be time to do at the moment.

Congregations that are not helped to have difficult conversations on race, class, and culture will react to such change in the most defensive and unhelpful ways. This is a story about race, white privilege, and the claims put upon the church by the gospel. Such reactions to issues of culture shift, as reported here, are not as uncommon as we like to imagine. In fact, they are on the increase in some areas of the country as birthrates and immigration are changing the face of our society. We see this clearly being played out on the political stage of our country as we are being challenged to reassess who we are as a nation of people and who we are as the church.

The board of the church grudgingly agreed to the study called for by the minister. Five members undertook the task of gathering data on demographic trends and the current reality of the congregation, including membership, attendance, and financial viability. They engaged in biblical reflection and prayer. They also addressed some difficult questions: "Where will our new members come from in the future? What do we need to do to attract new people? What do we need to change about ourselves and the focus of our ministry?" The report back to the board and congregation contained specific recommendations, including a change in the staffing model to add a minister of color and meaningful changes in programming and worship. The meeting at which the report was presented was well attended, even by members still on the rolls who had moved away and were no longer active. Their attendance, it turned out, was an organized effort to ensure that there would be enough votes to defeat the proposals, which they accomplished by a wide margin.

When a congregation is under stress or perceives itself to be under attack, it is the most inopportune time to raise these difficult issues. In hindsight, it would have been helpful if the congregation could have discussed neighborhood trends before the shock of change presented itself. Fear, racial bias, and anger that the minister was trying to "take their church away from them" set the course for this congregation's future. In a matter of a few years, the remnant of the white church dispersed and turned the facility over to a Latino congregation.

Lessons from This Case Study

- Even change that could ensure institutional health for the long term can be rejected if it challenges fundamental values and long-standing and unquestioned biases.
- Biblical mandates and theological framing are often insufficient motivators in the face of the emotional content of change in faith communities.
- Timing and time are critical factors in moving an organization through difficult change. In this case, there was not enough time for this congregation to adjust to a new reality, to turn

the corner and work through the issues of race, culture, and sense of calling before declining beyond a point of possible recovery. It is often the case that a congregation will deny or avoid significant change until the opportunity for renewed vitality passes them by.

- We cannot change the system without changing the norms. If you change the norms, you will likely not get rewarded because you are asking people to behave differently. In this case the norms of welcome did not include the children and families of color in this increasingly diverse neighborhood.
- Change often feels like a repudiation or rejection of how we have done things in the past or of what we value. In this case, the prospect of welcoming new people into the congregation posed a threat to the congregation's identity rather than an opportunity to embrace its community. The congregation felt that the values of the community were at odds with their values. "They are not like us." In fact, there were numerous values held in common. The desire for respect and safety, for a good education for their children, for the basics of health, adequate housing and meaningful work to support their families—all these were shared values. When we see the "other" as not like us, we are rejecting the possibility of relationship and using unsubstantiated and stereotypical views to justify our lack of engagement.

Nostalgia is the enemy of needed change. The harking back to a former time is appealing to some when faced with difficult change. In the many conversations I have had with congregational leaders, there is a deep connection to the history and culture of the faith community. Memories are strong for longtime members, and when they are attached to the personal story of one's spiritual journey, those memories call forth an allegiance to the past and how things were then. I have heard congregants wistfully express their grief and sense of loss for all the ways the world has changed, and inevitably they will suggest reinstituting programs and activities that once held the attention of members but are no longer effective in holding the congregation together, let alone in reaching new people.

When added to the "culture of memories," this culture of nostalgia alongside the reality of a growing population of ethnic, racial, and cultural diversity leaves many congregations feeling lost or in a state of denial about their current reality. Dwindling members and budget shortfalls create stress as the congregation closes in on itself. These congregations tend to do the things they know how to do, are comfortable doing, or like to do, even though those things have nothing to do with what needs to be done.

A Case Study of Culture Shift

Resistance is normal and should be expected whenever meaningful change is initiated. The greater the change and the more emotional the content of the change, the more heightened will be the resistance.

Consider a second case study: When one congregation determined to make changes in their worship life by adding artistic elements, they did so in an intentional and effective way, and they anticipated and planned for resistance. They held structured focus groups to hear members express their thoughts and feelings about the worship experience. One of the questions they asked was, "What experiences in worship have you had in other settings that you would like to experience here?" The responses to this question were key to understanding what was possible in pursuing their hope to make changes in the worship life of the congregation. Some said they love various genres of music from gospel to classical to jazz and other secular forms. They also indicated that they enjoyed puppets, drama, and movement in worship. Once the input was gathered, a report was made to the congregation of what was said. Many could recognize their thoughts and input in what was reported. The leadership then announced to the congregation that in the upcoming Lenten season the congregation would be invited into a spiritual journey that would include artistic elements in the Sunday morning worship celebration. They created a context for the changes, alerted the membership that this would be a Lenten spiritual focus, and created a time frame that was limited as an experiment. Before the Lenten season was over, members were saying, "We hope you have plans to continue these changes." A renewed spirit grew in the congregation as a result of renewed worship, which ultimately led to staff changes and strategic changes in other areas of the congregation's life.

Lessons from This Case Study

- Plan changes expecting resistance.
- Gather input and invite stories from stakeholders to build ownership.
- Create a container for change, in this case a specified period of time for this spiritual focus.
- Inform the congregation in advance: no surprises.
- Receive and act on feedback.
- Meaningful culture shift requires a realignment of resources (money and people).
- The change was institutionalized in the formation of a worship planning team to continue innovations in the worship experience.

Creating culture shift in the life of the congregation should be understood as an ongoing process. As changing circumstances call for new responses, the congregation will need to adapt and become more flexible in how it lives out its call and vision. Old answers will not resolve new challenges. A healthy congregational culture will exhibit a spirit of creativity, an expansive view of the future, and a capacity for thoughtful risk-taking.

Congregations will forgo needed change in order to preserve relationships and avoid conflict. If members are alienated by a proposed change, it can destabilize the system, especially if there is a fear that some may leave the faith community or withhold their support. The smaller the congregation, the more this dynamic is likely to present itself. When a congregation senses its vulnerability, when it is aware of a decline in attendance and is struggling to meet expenses, such realities often cause retreat from needed change, and the congregation can become risk averse rather than take on the task of revitalization or redevelopment, undertaking major change or culture shift.

Resistance to change should be understood as information, never simply as a contest for power or desire to thwart leadership. Resistance is often rooted in legitimate concerns and feelings. Resistance to change manifests in various forms:

1. When people are reasonably happy with things as they are, they will see no justification for change. "Why fix it if it isn't broken?" is a familiar expression of resistance. When people are invested in the status quo and benefitting from it, they will not see the need for making changes or acknowledge the institution's vulnerability. In change theory, it is sometimes necessary to introduce discomfort to create movement and the possibility of change.
2. Fear of the unknown is often a cause for resistance. Fear can paralyze. "What will be the outcomes of this change?" "What if it doesn't turn out as we hoped?" "What if this proposed change causes some of my friends to leave this church?" Fear is born of a sense of

vulnerability, the realization of our limitations, and that, ultimately, we are not in control and can offer no guarantees. Fear of failure is an honest reaction to any major change.

3. A lack of confidence and awareness that "we" might not be capable of effecting the change that is proposed can cause resistance. Systems might not want to embrace the hard work or deal with the emotional content of disruption. "Do we have what it takes to succeed?"

4. Resistance can be the result of ineffective communication. When people are not given adequate information or they sense information is being withheld and there is a lack of transparency, they resist. If there is a lack of trust in the system, or some stakeholders have not been part of the conversation and decision-making, they may hesitate to commit to the proposed change.

5. If there are unresolved issues in the congregation or a need for healing relationships, these issues will be serious obstacles to instituting change. It is sometimes the case that events in the past will be carried forward and resurface in the form of resistance to even the smallest change.

6. Stereotypes and unconscious bias can be operative on issues of diversity and inclusion. Some feelings and perceptions can be strongly held but not "owned" when they are at odds with the published values of the organization, yet they are strong influences in the system.

Reflections on the Dynamics of Change

1. If change is to occur there must be "enough" pain, discomfort, sense of urgency, and awareness of threat in the system to motivate the change. Pain needs hope to create possibilities; otherwise the system and the leaders become immobilized.

2. Leaders are rewarded for making people happy. By making people happy, you decrease the motivation for needed change. Leaders of change create "safety" rather than "comfort."

3. Systems will collude around answers that won't work in order to reduce discomfort and avoid change.

4. We tend to do the things we know how to do, are comfortable doing, and like to do even though they have nothing to do with what needs to be done.

5. Change often feels like a repudiation or rejection of how we have done things in the past or of what we value. Our response is often to keep doing the same things but differently rather than doing a truly new thing.

6. Systems are designed for the results they produce. To get a different result, you have to change the system. When you change part of any system, you affect the whole system. When the system does not produce the results we want, our natural response is to replace the leader.

7. When systems are not producing the results we want, we often make evaluative responses. Evaluative responses are received as a threat or as a judgment, leaving only two options: fight or flight. "Evaluation" goes to the reptilian part of the brain. "Description" goes to the part of the brain that allows for processing, reflection, and negotiation.

8. Some changes are "technical," and others are "adaptive":*
    - Technical—the application of known solutions to known problems. (A part in a piece of machinery fails, the problem is diagnosed, the part is replaced, and the machine works again.)
    - Adaptive—requires learning, experimentation, innovation to both define the issues and arrive at an appropriate response or often multiple responses. Adaptive work requires a change in values, beliefs, and behaviors. A problem-solving model does not work here.
9. We often avoid adaptive work because it is more difficult and we feel we do not have the tools to "fix" the problem. We avoid this work by
    - Holding on to past assumptions
    - Blaming authority
    - Scapegoating
    - Externalizing the enemy
    - Denying the problem
    - Jumping to conclusions, prescribing the answer
    - Finding a distracting issue, creating a distraction
    - Assassinating the leader when things are not resolved quickly
10. The deepest adaptive work to be done is *in* the leader. The interior work of the leader is the most important work to be done. Leaders need to ask:
    - What change must I make personally if I am to help my institution do the right thing?
    - What will keep me from making those changes?
    - What help or resources do I need for this personal adaptive work?
    - What is my "learning" agenda for self and system?
11. A key task of the leader is to be able to "read" their system and describe it.
12. Leaders exhibit integrity, transparency, respect, trust, and empathy for followers. Leaders are learners and teachers.
13. We cannot change the system without changing the norms. If you change the norms, you will likely not get rewarded because you are asking people to behave differently.
14. Change requires listening and learning, not fixed positions; a sense of hope; sustained attention to issues over time; and a sense of continuity with the past.
15. Theology of Change:
    - God creates and re-creates, makes all things new, moves us toward transformation.
    - God is a change advocate.
    - God brings order out of chaos and chaos out of order.
    - Change is normative.
    - Genesis 32—Jacob gets a new name and a new identity.
    - Romans 12—Be transformed.
    - Revelation 21—I make all things new.

*For more information on managing change, see Ronald A. Heifetz, *Leadership without Easy Answers* (Cambridge, MA: Belknap Press, 1994) and John P. Kottler, *Leading Change* (Cambridge, MA: Harvard Business Review Press, 2012).

Force Field Analysis

One process for assessing the possibility of change is known as the *Force Field Analysis.* This model was developed by social scientist Kurt Lewin to demonstrate that organizations and people are not static. Lewin makes the case that any current reality is the result of a dynamic balance of forces pushing in opposite directions. Some of these forces are called *driving forces* and put pressure on organizations to change. Other forces, called *restraining forces,* pressure organizations not to change. Lewin asserted that when an organization is in a relatively stable state, the forces for and against change are in relative equilibrium. He saw this as a *quasi-static equilibrium.* A system in this state is usually motivated to change by some unforeseen circumstance or set of circumstances. For our purposes, this might be a congregation that is aware of a demographic shift in the community or that a few visitors of another ethnicity have attended worship. This may prompt a few leaders to raise this observation at the next board meeting. To create needed change and move the system from *quasi-static equilibrium* toward change, one must achieve two things simultaneously: increase the driving forces and decrease the restraining forces. This is illustrated by the following example. Do your own Force Field Analysis by using the blank chart on page 34.

The Goal: To Move the Congregation toward Greater Diversity and Inclusion

Driving Forces	Restraining Forces
The community is in transition, becoming more diverse ethnically.	Members blame new residents for decline in their property values.
Current membership is in decline.	Unexpressed fear of strangers
We aren't meeting our budget.	We have reserve funds to stay as we are.
Some leaders see the need to build relationships with the community.	Longtime members want to preserve the status quo.
Without attracting new members, the congregation could dissolve in five years.	The board wants the minister to give more time to visit the sick and shut-ins.
We have a theological mandate to welcome the stranger.	Unconscious bias and denial of situation.

FORCE FIELD ANALYSIS

Generate your own Force Field Analysis as it applies to the change goal of becoming more diverse ethnically or culturally. If the analysis does not indicate readiness for change, then the correct question to ask is, "What must we do to help the congregation get ready for needed change?" rather than resigning the faith community to doing nothing.

Driving Forces	Restraining Forces

The next step in the force field analysis is to identify actions to take to maximize the driving forces and minimize the constraining forces. What might be *important, real,* or *probable* actions to take? In the case of the stated goal of this exercise, actions one might consider are the following:

- Identifying potential allies in the congregation and conducting one-on-one conversations.
- Gathering additional information on projected demographic change.
- Easing congregational anxiety by building cross-cultural relationships.
- Asking your leaders to read the stories of other congregations that have become more diverse.
- Inviting outside expertise to assist in the process.

Though congregations tend to be tradition-bound institutions, there is adequate scriptural foundation for a theology of change. God creates and re-creates, makes all things new, and moves us toward personal and corporate transformation. In this sense, God is a change advocate, and change (transformation) is a normative value in the faith tradition. In Genesis 32, Jacob gets a new name and a new identity. In Romans 12, we are called to be transformed, made new; and in Revelations 21 God asserts: "I am making all things new." A static life of faith is an impoverished life of faith. A community of faith that is not always moving forward, growing, learning, and changing has misunderstood the call and claim of the gospel. A congregation that has quietly closed the door on needed change, disregarded the opportunity to welcome the stranger, and kept itself safe from discomfort and the unfamiliar has not awakened to the God who not only welcomes change but also instigates it. God brings chaos out of our cherished order.

Review Stage 2 of the Pentecost Paradigm

– Have you conducted a Force Field Analysis? What have you discerned from this exercise?

_____

_____

– What is the theological frame for change that results in becoming a multiracial, multicultural congregation?

_____

_____

– Have leaders been prepared for some members to leave the church?

_____

_____

– Where is resistance on display, and how are leaders managing this dynamic?

_____

_____

PREPARING FOR CHANGE MANAGEMENT

Review the information about the Dynamics of Change (pp. 31–32), then answer the following questions to prepare yourselves to manage the changes ahead for your congregation and the potential resistance to them.

1. Discuss changes the congregation has experienced in the past. What happened during those experiences, and how did the congregation address the natural resistance that accompanies change?

2. What has been learned from previous significant changes in the congregation that inform how to lead the next change initiative?

3. What are some changes your congregation may need to consider in the near future? What are the compelling reasons to work for these changes?

4. What is the theological frame for "norming" change in your congregation?

5. As leaders, what will need to change about how we lead in this time and in our place?

Chapter 4

Creating Congregational Identity

*C*ongregational identity describes our sense of who we are in our relationship to each other, to the community around us, and to the faith tradition of which we are a part. Identity is shaped by the stories we tell about ourselves and those others tell about us. Our identity is shaped by relationships, history, ritual, shared values, and our picture of the future. It is informed by decisions we have made, testing we have endured, and by our faithfulness to the gospel. Identity is informed by our sense of calling and purpose.

Congregations become racially and culturally diverse with purposefulness and intentionality. In our experience, most congregations hold a self-perception that they are warm and welcoming, safe and loving communities of faith. They have evolved patterns, habits, and norms that are practiced both consciously and unconsciously. Many congregations continue to behave in ways shaped by their past rather than create new norms that support a vision for the future. When congregations reflect on their identity, who they are, they tend to use language that describes what they value about their current circumstances rather than thinking aspirationally about who they are striving to become. The question "Who are we?" often prompts responses such as *We are mission minded. We are generous. We are welcoming. We are a loving community. We are Bible believing.* When pressed for the meaning of these identifiers, congregations will often confess, *We support denominational missions. We support our church's budget. In reality, we don't really welcome everyone. We love each other. And we have Bible study every week for anyone who wants to attend.*

Additionally, congregations rarely ask themselves, "How does the larger community around us describe who we are?" When I ask this latter question of leaders in congregations, they have responded with such answers as these: *They think we are the wealthy "mink coat" church* or *They say we are the white church on the corner* or *Nobody really knows us but us.* In too many instances they report that people in the community have been heard to say, "I didn't know that church was still open."

Shaping an identity that is authentic and aspirational, energizing and visionary is a critical step in effecting a culture shift in the congregation. Can the congregation reach agreement on who they are aspiring to become, or where God is calling them to go now? And the bigger question is, Are they "behaving" this aspiration and this call?

In a society that reinforces the value of monoracial, monocultural groupings, we become acculturated to this as normative. Of course, there are historical reasons for this; however, it may be time for all of us to question what is normative in view of the fact that such separation has left us not knowing our neighbors, being afraid of strangers, and feeling isolated from one another. It is precisely at this point that the church can offer an alternative to the tenacious divisions in this country by becoming truly welcoming, diverse, and inclusive faith communities and modeling for the larger society what the beloved community looks like.

Congregational identity is shaped out of its history, its challenges, victories, and aspirations. It is also shaped out of a congregation's understanding of its faith tradition, its spiritual journey, and its sense of God's calling. Remembering its history can be a real asset in shaping its future direction. History can also be a hindrance. It would disturb some of us and embarrass others to realize how many congregations have a history of support for the KKK that has never been discussed among the members yet haunts its identity to this day. Too many churches in both the North and the South provided safe harbor and generous inclusion for Klan members or members of the John Birch Society, where they were respected leaders and officers. This history is buried in shame and never discussed, partly because the attitudes at the core of these groups still reside in these congregations and still contribute to their identity and shape their worldview and their relationships with their communities.

I (John) once lived in a community where the Klan had announced they would be holding a rally. I met with the local clergy organization to ask what plans they were developing in response. They sheepishly offered that they had discussed the matter and decided that the best response was to ignore the Klan, to do nothing. Feeling some urgency to have a public response of opposition, I pushed them to take a stand. Finally they agreed to hold a prayer vigil concurrent with the Klan rally. Later I was told that they were concerned they would alienate some of their members if they made "too much of a fuss" against the Klan.

When it comes to welcoming the stranger, providing hospitality, and creating safe space for newcomers of a different ethnicity, the congregation's spiritual maturity and vision for its future would ideally be carefully discerned before the first visitor of another ethnicity or culture appeared at the door. Otherwise, as it happened in one congregation, the first visitor may be told by the greeter at the front door, "The church you are looking for is on the other side of town." This shows the importance of being aware of demographic changes in the community and being ready to receive the newcomers. I have visited some congregations where I was unknown to the members and felt the chill of suspicion and lack of welcome as though I had entered a private club and forgot my membership card. I should add that these were almost entirely white churches, and I am white. I have had the opposite experience when visiting black, Korean, and Latino churches, where I was the only white person, yet warmly welcomed. This is a typical story and is accounted for by the minority community having to learn how to navigate the majority white world, while whites have had no need to know how to navigate the world of people of color. For a white person, not knowing how nor perceiving the need to relate to communities of color is a manifestation of white privilege.

Getting Ready for a Multiracial, Multicultural Identity

Readiness is an important issue in any congregation that has the opportunity to reach an increasingly diverse community. Readiness is indicated by open conversation about the demographic shift in the community as it is happening. Worship begins to introduce a wider variety of music. A diversity of leadership is invited to participate in worship. More and more people from the growing population are partners in the development of programs that support their needs and interests. The congregation is inviting.

Even congregations that are already racially and culturally diverse need to pay attention to readiness. This is illustrated by the story of one multicultural congregation with a membership of white, African American, Caribbean, and African diaspora who remained largely passive about a growing Latino population, even though they hosted a community educational program for Latino children in their building. Over the course of twenty years the Latino population grew to nearly 40 percent of the community's total population. During this time of population growth, the congregation built no bridges, partnerships, or common cause with the Latino community. Now being so far behind the curve, they are unlikely to communicate sincerity or credibility in any effort to relate to or partner with this community. This congregation will now need to find a focus for engagement that begins to change their story in relationship to the Latino community and has no strings attached—including that the trade-off for their efforts be the expectation of new members from the Latino community. At the time of this writing, this congregation is in discussion about making a commitment to support a citywide literacy program, largely aimed at Latino children, and partnering with others in the community in supporting the just treatment of immigrant families under threat of being separated by deportation.

Getting ready to become a multicultural, multiracial congregation is very important; it is like traveling to a new or unfamiliar place. By discussing the following questions, you may gain insight into steps to take toward greater diversity.

THE JOURNEY TOWARD MULTIRACIAL IDENTITY

1. What do we need to pack for this journey? Not only what equipment we must put in our suitcase, but also "What is our baggage?" What assumptions, perceptions, fears and expectations might we have about the place we will travel to?

2. What is the "climate"? Will we find it hot or chilly, and will we dress accordingly? Can we exhibit flexibility rather than expecting the new environment to accommodate us?

3. What is our itinerary? What stops will we make on the trip? Who are the people we want to speak to?

4. What community organizations do we want to learn about?

5. Do we have the proper documentation or passport—that is, do we have credibility? Have we indicated in our public materials (worship bulletin, newsletter, Web site, and signage) that we are explicitly open to diversity?

6. Have we learned any of the local language, and can we listen carefully and learn? Can we "speak" inclusion by informing the larger community of worship observances in Black History month, MLK remembrance, or Cinco de Mayo?

7. Do we know the history of the people we will engage? Do we know the values, hopes, and aspirations we share in common? What do we have in common?

8. Do we know something of the culture to give us clues about how to behave? What are the cultural norms for communication? What behaviors communicate respect?

9. Do we need a guide, someone who can help us find our way? Who do we know that can introduce us to the local people? Who might be our partners, and who might we invite to meet with us before we start out on this journey?

Once a community begins to change ethnically or culturally, and a church has not engaged new residents in the community soon after they arrive, it is extremely difficult to establish meaningful relationships later on. A delay in welcoming the stranger raises suspicions about the congregation's openness in the minds of the newcomers. This passivity communicates rejection and unwelcome that is difficult to overcome. Setting the terms for a relationship rather than collaborating, supporting, and celebrating what this new population has to offer is a "white" or "majority" behavior. Hanging out a sign that says "All Are Welcome" is viewed with cynicism when there is no tangible sign of genuine collaboration and no time invested in listening deeply to the aspirations, fears, and joys of those we say we want to reach. Developing a program "for them" is not likely to produce the results we desire.

One congregation involved in a strategic planning process indicated that they viewed the growing ethnic population as holding different values from their own. For this reason the congregation saw no justification for building bridges to that community of newcomers. When pressed on this perception, they came to see that the congregation held many values in common with those newcomers, including the values of a safe environment for their children, quality education, adequate housing, meaningful work, and finding a faith community as a spiritual home. When we "other" the stranger, we are blind to all the ways "we" and "they" are much alike.

No matter what is published about their identity, congregations will be known to the larger community for the story they behave. Congregations behave who they are all the time. Even when a congregation does not reflect on and agree to their identity and intentionally behave who they aspire to be, their identity is still clear to the larger community. For example, it speaks loudly when a faith community is silent on issues of injustice. When a congregation does not address controversial issues; when the minister does not preach a challenging word and the congregation is quick with criticism if she does; when no prayers are offered on behalf of the oppressed; when the words *sexual orientation*, *racial justice*, or *economic disparity* are never spoken—all of this signals the congregation's identity. It is important that the congregation shape its identity to be true to the gospel, authentic in the current moment, and relatable to potential new constituents.

For example, Middle Collegiate Church behaves its identity as a radically welcoming and inclusive community. This is consistently displayed on its Web site, in its presence in the public square, in the diversity of the staff and volunteers, and in congregational life. For many years Middle Church has had a float in the annual Heritage of Pride March, supported the Black Lives Matter movement, and demonstrated against gun violence. This has been key to its ability to attract a new and diverse flow of visitors who often become constituents and then members and volunteers. We will say more about behaving identity in the public square in chapter 10.

Alongside issues of congregational identity is the need for the congregation to heighten its visibility in the community. An oft-repeated story is of churches that appear to be closed or are dying due to their inactivity or the outward appearance of their facility. They become "invisible" to the passersby. The front entrance may appear imposing, with heavy wooden doors usually locked and unused during the week because the members know what side door or rear door to use. Visitors can feel locked out. It is just as likely that those in search of a church home will visit the Web site first, the other "front door." Try the exercise below to try to see your church as newcomers see it.

HOW'S YOUR FRONT DOOR?

Your Virtual Door

1. Does your Web site communicate welcome to a diverse population?

2. Can strangers find information and images that they can relate to, such as sermon titles, guest speakers, special programs, or stories that indicate multicultural welcome?

3. Does your Web site show causes you support, partnerships with which you engage, or advocacy you provide? Such attention to details can speak to the congregation's identity and raise its visibility in the community.

4. Explore the Web site of your closest neighbor or a church that you perceive as growing and thriving. How do they tell their story?

5. What can you find on their Web site that indicates who they are? What is their identity?

Your Physical Door

1. Stand across the street from your church on a Wednesday evening. What do you see? Wooden door? Iron gate? Do you look "open for business"?

2. Drive around the community and look at other church buildings. How are these buildings communicating welcome and accessibility? How does the facility itself tell a story about the faith community's identity?

3. Do you imagine that passersby even notice that your church, a building they pass every day, is a church and is open and serves the community? How would they know this is the case just by looking?

Some congregations have become sophisticated about marketing principles. At Middle Church, marketing—or telling our story—is the language used for what others call evangelism. The story we tell is the redemptive story of the gospel, and our own story of justice making, people serving, and spiritual homemaking. We invite people to join a movement, not a congregation. We ask them to support this movement with their time, talents, and money. The movement is a movement to make the world what God intended it to be, more loving and just, caring for the least among us, and ensuring that everyone has enough. We respect the faith traditions of others and leave behind the requirements of creedal affirmations, preferring to create a faith community where participants are invited to extend and receive grace, touch and experience the Holy, and discover the spiritual in themselves and others.

This is the identity communicated and "marketed" by this congregation that speaks of everyone being welcomed just as they are as they come through the door. This identity is expressed in every way possible, in music, preaching, education, social action, community involvement, space usage, partnerships, news and program print and TV media, Huff Post, Web site and video, and yes, Twitter.

A congregation's identity must be clear, compelling, and consistent. It must also be expressed in multiple ways and in multiple "languages" for various audiences, young and old, ethnically diverse constituencies and across cultures. A congregation's identity cannot be a well-kept secret. It must be a declaration that calls others to its high purpose and bold vision.

〜〜〜〜〜〜〜

Review Stage 2 of the Pentecost Paradigm

– Is the congregation in conversation about their identity, who they aspire to become?

_____

_____

_____

_____

_____

– What early steps are being taken to help the congregation talk about diverse community?

_____

_____

_____

_____

WHAT'S OUR IDENTITY?

Discuss these questions as a group. Would people outside your congregation give the same answers about you?

1. What are we known for?

2. What do we promote as our "signature ministries," those commitments that identify who we are as a faith community?

3. What is our "brand," those words, phrases, or statements that describe our essence, our heart, our aspirations? (This should not be your denominational affiliation.)

4. What are the "verbs," the action words that describe us as a community of faith, and how do these verbs connect with the lives of those we want to reach?

Chapter 5

Building Capacity

*W*hile there are general categories of competence and gifts for ministry, there are particular attributes, knowledge, and skills needed for ministry in multicultural and multiracial settings. These settings exhibit dynamics and complexities not found in monocultural and monoethnic congregations. Sensitivities of language, history, interpretation of texts, and relational dynamics require the ability of leadership to hold diverse constituent groups in community. In this regard, leadership development through training and coaching is essential to the effort for both the clergy and the laity. The following are key capacities we feel are needed to do this work.

Leaders in congregations moving toward greater diversity possess *a deep understanding of the story of race and culture* in America. Having command of the history of peoples of color in the story of America is important to leadership credibility and effectiveness. From the genocide of native peoples to the middle passage and the rise of slavery, reconstruction and Jim Crow, the treatment of Chinese laborers and Japanese internment, the demonization of Mexicans, hate crimes against Muslims, the Holocaust, and the recent resurgence of anti-Semitism—white supremacy and xenophobia have created an atmosphere of violence and division that has risen to a fever pitch at different times along the arc of our nation's story. When we understand that the doctrine of manifest destiny, for example, was little more than a political construct to justify the seizure of land from native peoples and a strategy to unify the continent under the governance of white European descendants and tame the land through the enslavement of Africans, then we begin to grasp the backstory of race in America. It is not the romanticized, revisionist account of history most of us have been taught but rather the suppressed story as people of color would tell it. Understanding the effects of colonialism in Africa, Asia, and Central and South America, and knowing the driving forces behind human migration patterns—all that is invaluable to reading the hopes, dreams, fears, and aspirations of newcomers from many backgrounds, religious traditions, and cultural settings.

In the story of all of us, knowing the crosscurrents of cultures and the dynamics of race matters. It matters that we know how we got here, in this present moment. The racial reconciliation so many of us aspire to effect in our country is not possible without excavating these stories and understanding the challenges and the victories, the wounding and the healing, and the yet unfulfilled hopes and dreams for "a more perfect union." Our treasured and varied faith traditions reside in the context of our nation's story, and it is often the case that our faith traditions have helped shape the nation's story. Confessionally, we also recognize that the faith community has been influenced and infected by the nation's story in confusing and compromising ways. It is sometimes difficult to discuss openly in the congregation the tension between the call to national allegiance and to simultaneously honor the claims of the faith tradition. We readily see, then, that the nation's story and the stories of religion in America are inextricably interwoven. Spiritual leaders need to understand all of these stories in order to articulate a vision for a healed and whole world and to create a safe container for healthy diversity.

Leaders demonstrate *the ability to articulate a personal vision* for their lives, their ministry, and the world. Spiritual leaders called to this work are possessed by a vision for a healed world. It is a vision that transcends cultural norms of clan, tribe, and nationality. It is a vision striving for understanding, hungering for hope, and manifesting diverse human community. It is a vision unimpeded by fear, distraction, or by what is thought to be possible. These leaders can articulate a prophetic social critique and a vision for the world as God intended it to be. They invite others to this vision and occupy space in the public square as well as in the sanctuary to promote it. In one-on-one conversations, in small groups, in worship, in adult educational settings, on the church's Web site, and in blogs and editorials, the vision is repeatedly articulated.

Recently while sitting in a train station and waiting to board, I (John) struck up a conversation with a woman traveling with her family to Baltimore. In the course of the conversation, she expressed her fear that the world was acting out the prophecies of the book of Revelation and that things were heading to a cataclysmic end time. She went on to say that she was glad she was "saved" and that all that mattered to her now was that she and her family's salvation were assured. This personal vision is unintentionally cynical; in my opinion it is wrongheaded theologically and the most impoverished expression of the Christian faith. If we substitute a vision of a healed world with a self-obsessed vision of personal salvation, we surrender hope, deny human goodness, and reject the notion that the world is worthy of redemption and that we all have responsibility for the common good. From this woman's vantage point, we need do nothing to work for radical change. We have only to protect our own interests while waiting for the world to go to hell in a handbasket. This is the kind of vision that lives in the hearts of some of our congregants. Leaders need the capacity to articulate a vision that counteracts this one.

Leaders also exhibit *courage* to effect change in the face of resistance and have the capacity for risk taking. Spiritual leaders are undeterred by opposing forces that seek to derail a moral agenda or that are committed to the status quo. They welcome others to join in enacting a grander vision. They stay the course when under pressure to modulate, delay, or abandon the work of advancing a vision for a more just and compassionate world. They are capable of sustaining losses, grieving, and regrouping to resume the work. They can take appropriate risks needed to honor their vision, attract partners, form alliances, and effect change. It is the nature of moral courage to stand for justice and work for peace and reconciliation in the face of controversy and conflict. It is the nature of moral courage to exhibit compassion and an ethic of love in the toxic atmosphere of national divisions and long-standing animosities. It is the nature of moral courage to insist that the poor, lost, and left out be lifted up, spoken for, and protected from the disregard of the powerful and that the common good be our common aspiration.

Leaders exhibit *emotional intelligence*. Research into the field of emotional intelligence has concluded that self-knowledge and self-awareness are key factors in giving exceptional leadership in any organization. This is especially true in checking our unconscious biases in multiracial, multicultural settings. Without this capacity, it is nearly impossible to empathize with another person. It is this capacity for empathy, for reading and acknowledging the feelings of others, that *Primal Leadership* authors call "resonate leadership."[1] This capacity frees us for creativity, builds authentic relationships, and allows for truth telling.

Knowing ourselves, including what Parker Palmer calls our "shadow" side,[2] also means claiming and giving voice to our unspoken hopes, embracing the vision that will not let us go, that haunts our sleep and challenges our disbelief. Such self-knowledge can carry us beyond our fears and allow us to traverse the open ground of experimentation and be holy and wholly vulnerable. In this vulnerability leaders portray the strength that builds trust, attracts followers, and helps focus the energy of the community around purposeful action.

It is not enough, however, for us to confront our shadow side. We must also live in the light. It is this latter task that can be the most terrifying of all. To step out and announce the dream in the midst of the community requires uncommon courage. It is the mark of spiritual leadership that we have the capacity to confront the dream stealers among us, those who pick the spiritual pockets of the faith community, who limit its vision and diminish its resources. When a spiritual leader allows the inappropriate and controlling behavior of others to go unchecked and unchallenged, they lose power and credibility.

It is important that we have the *spiritual strength* to issue a challenge to the faith community and that we are sufficiently self-differentiated to stand against the fears of others and not be overcome by them. We come to this deep self-knowledge through the sometimes rough-and-tumble engagement with the world around us, and we are aided in our pursuit of self-knowledge by our own self-reflection and the observations and feedback of others. Those who see the need for deep self-knowledge are working with a spiritual director, coach, or therapist as a resource in keeping their balance, maintaining authenticity, and setting healthy boundaries for this work.

Leaders have a keen *understanding of their prophetic role*. It is the prophetic role to read the dominant culture in light of the faith tradition and to describe the discord and disconnect between them. The prophetic voice is not employed to announce revisions in the current reality, but to announce a new reality altogether. By its very nature, the prophetic role requires the prophet to be fully immersed in the life of the larger culture and fully immersed in the faith tradition. It is this complete identification with both the culture and the faith tradition that subjects the prophet to the grief and anguish of a faith community distanced from God and at the same time qualifies them as the authentic voice of hope. It is the prophet who must balance high tension simultaneously on two fronts: first, with the dominant culture, which often demonstrates a predisposition to a hostile response to the prophet's message; and second, with the faith community, which is often ambivalent at best about the requirements of faithfulness.

The prophetic task is carried out both individually and corporately. The faith community is called to counter the prevailing culture and serve as the transformational element in the larger plan of universal redemption. In the midst of a culture some would describe as driven by the undercurrents of greed, nihilism, and exclusion, the faith community stands for an alternative reality of hope, healing, and freedom from cultural and spiritual tyrannies. In an age of technology it is necessary for prophetic witness to engage justice issues in the public square as well as in the congregation. This may include writing blogs or editorials; addressing the city council, zoning board, or school board; or speaking at public events, including those designed for public protest.

The spiritual leader is *both teacher and student*. Reaching beyond the most common expectations for clergy leaders as "Bible study teacher" is a rich and diverse range of topics and resources available for the edification of believers. In multicultural, multiracial congregational settings, the role of leader as educator is even more essential. It invites the congregation into structured conversations where norms for dealing with difficult conversations are made clear and safe space is created for honest dialogue. In the case of Middle Church, we have offered adult study groups on "Erasing Racism," "Exploring Race, Class, and Culture," and "Race, Grace, and the Reign of God," all of which invite participants to explore their own stories regarding the formative messages and lessons they received regarding race while growing up in this society. Additionally, we have convened a Racial Healing Task Force, which has committed to a yearlong process of shared learning to engage in truth telling, storytelling, research, and the evolution of a learning design for others who want to work at issues of race, racism, and white supremacy. We have asked participants to learn the history of the nation from its founding to the institution of slavery, to Jim Crow, the Civil Rights Movement to Ferguson,[3] and the current movement to challenge the manifestations of racism and white supremacy. These leaders develop other leaders by expanding knowledge, giving language and voice to discuss difficult issues, and creating a community where this work is ongoing and normalized. In our view every congregation, regardless of location or demographic makeup, is called to conversation on issues of race, class, and gender identity.

The spiritual leader in a multicultural, multiracial setting is called to provide opportunities for the members of the faith community to deepen their understanding of each other and of the issues impacting the world around them. These leaders must see themselves as students of race, culture, and the dynamics of white privilege and white supremacy in order to be effective in the work of healing and reconciliation.

These leaders are *community organizers and activists*. Effective leaders in multiracial, multicultural faith communities are required to possess the skills needed not only to organize their own congregation but also the ability to analyze issues, network with others, and organize the larger community on issues of social justice and the common good. Without active engagement with the larger community and a willingness to put oneself in the public square, advocating for those without a voice, the children, the poor, the hungry, and the left out—without such activism, the witness of the faith community will be greatly diminished. This is especially true for diverse congregations, which serve as a model for people standing with others and their concerns when those concerns may not immediately impact themselves. We do this for each other. We march for Black Lives Matter, we sign petitions for the rights of Muslims, and we advocate for LGBT justice and inclusion. We know it matters to our members and our constituents, and it matters to our community that they see our congregation parading down Fifth Avenue in the Pride March. Multicultural, multiracial faith communities walk their talk of inclusion, equal rights, and justice for all.

Spiritual leaders are able to *manage conflict and difference*. Understanding the sources of conflict and possessing an awareness of our own biases are attributes necessary for effective leadership in these congregations. Sharing power across racial and cultural boundaries, not letting differences become polarizing, keeping communication open and healthy, and ensuring mutuality in accountability—these are helpful norms in diverse settings. When dealing with multiple cultures in a faith community, it is likely that there will be differing norms for how to best resolve a conflict. Leaders have a responsibility to understand these differing norms and take them into account in addressing differences. Establishing behavioral covenants before a significant conflict arises will help set boundaries for engagement and create safe space for problem solving.

These spiritual leaders are intentional in *developing other leaders*. In a congregational setting, leadership development must move beyond the categories of standing committees and the exercise of filling mandatory slots in an organizational structure. As the clergy are expected to engage in continuing education, so members of the faith community should have the expectation of their own spiritual, intellectual, and emotional development. Opportunities for learning and growth are important to the health of the institution. Leaders have been trained in the story of race and culture, understanding the dynamics of change, how to manage conflict and difference, and how to set healthy norms for group effectiveness. They carry with them the vision of the congregation and are purposeful to enact that vision, and they make space for others to exert leadership and offer their knowledge and expertise to expand the impact and influence of the congregation. Leadership is diverse and encourages inclusion. True leaders know when to step aside and mentor new people with new ideas to step forward.

Trusted, transparent, competent, informed, and flexible leadership in multicultural, multiracial congregational settings is central to the health and witness of these ministries. Given the realities of a demographic sea change, heightening racial and cultural tensions across the country, and the increase in hate crimes, every person in roles of spiritual leadership—both clergy and laity—must view their own continuing education in cultural competency and the dynamics of racism and unconscious bias as vital to their effectiveness, whether or not they are in a multicultural, multiracial setting.

Activities toward Capacity Building

The following is a selected list of capacities reviewed in this chapter, with ideas for developing them further with your team. Take time to review all the capacities discussed here and assess next steps to take in strengthening leadership in your congregation.

1. Deepen our understanding of the story of race and culture.
    - Read and discuss Ta-Nehisi Coates's book *Between the World and Me* or some other work that invites conversation about race.
    - Brainstorm sermon topics that could lift up issues of race and culture.
    - Host conversations open to the community with special presenters discussing issues of race, culture, immigration, or Christian-Muslim dialogue.
    - Discuss the importance of becoming more diverse as a faith community.
2. Educate our members on issues of diversity.
    - Watch the film *Crash*, or another film, and discuss the issues raised.
    - As a monocultural congregation, discuss how race is an issue that is relevant in our predominantly white community.
    - Partner with a congregation of another ethnicity to improve relationships.
    - Establish an ongoing adult class that explores ethnicity, class, and culture.
3. Determine our prophetic role.
    - Explore the theological/biblical roots of your role as leaders in the larger community.

- Plan a short-term study of justice issues relevant to your local setting and formulate a process to help your congregation become more involved in addressing justice issues.
- Discuss how to raise our profile as advocates for justice and the common good in our community.

4. Develop other leaders.
- Develop a process for orientation of new leaders that includes heightening their awareness of issues of race and culture.
- Add to our church library some resources and books related to these topics.
- Institute quarterly training events for prospective new leaders and for those currently in leadership roles.

Review Stage 2 of the Pentecost Paradigm

- How is the congregation intentionally building capacity for multiracial, multicultural ministry? What resources are you using? PBS? Coates's book? A film series? The movie "13th"?

- What training is being provided? What structured conversations are happening?

- Have one-on-one conversations with key leaders to communicate and test your vision for a more multiracial congregation.

- Send your leaders to visit congregations that have successfully navigated the transition from monoracial to multiracial. Evaluate their worship and plan worship that reflects best practices.

Chapter 6

Cultivating Community

*T*he work of building multiracial, multicultural communities is both exciting and difficult. I am convinced that the difficulty is why many congregations shy away from this transformational work. In fact, there is still thinking afoot that growing a congregation is most easily done in monocultural contexts. The Rev. Dr. Martin Luther King Jr. often observed the segregated nature of most congregations. Though there has been progress made in this regard, the authors of *United by Faith* observe that only 7.5 percent of America's 300,000 Christian congregations are multiracial, defined as having at least 20 percent nonmajority in the congregation.[1]

When rethinking church today, it is important to go forward by recalling the past. The earliest churches were multiracial and multicultural. When Jewish people from all the known world were gathered in Jerusalem for Shavuot—commemorating the giving of the law to Moses—they encountered a miracle of communication and community building. Despite the fact that the Galilean disciples were testifying to the amazing grace of God's love and power in Aramaic, all of those who gathered, from Cyrene to Libya, heard the story of God's deeds of power in their own language! In the midst of stunning ethnic and cultural diversity, the story of God's love of humanity created community amid diversity, and the church was born.

So how did people who claim to love God end up fearful of diversity? We know that the church is part of the world, and the world can be a fearful place. Human beings fear that which they do not understand; we take aim at otherness as we seek the comfort of our own kind. And of course, in a racist culture, congregations can be racist.

Given my commitment to antiracist work, I (Jacqui) approached graduate school while questioning the development of racial identity. Since there is only one race—human—how is so-called race constructed? It is a narrative constructed in history, perhaps first asserted by Thomas Jefferson's suspicion that there is something "inferior" about the Negro.[2] Over the arc of global history, pseudo-science asserted the superiority of whites (so-called Caucasians) and the inferiority of blacks. This construct lead to the justification of slavery, the institution of Jim Crow in America, apartheid in South Africa, and ultimately to segregation in American congregations. I am convinced that the myth of white supremacy and the racism that it insinuates in our national story is a lie, a false story. And since the story is constructed, we can change it. I am also clear that multiracial, multicultural communities can change the story.

Multiracial, multicultural communities of faith give us the opportunity to practice being human together; they allow us, I like to say, to rehearse the reign of God here on earth. Deeply committed to changing the story on race in America, I wrote my doctoral dissertation in 2004 as an ethnographic and psychological study of five ethnically and culturally diverse congregations and their leaders. In *Authoring Stories for the New Religious Frontier*,[3] I sought to discover how congregational leaders cultivate multiracial, multicultural communities. What is the nature of the care they offer? How do they nurture their systems and train their congregations to live with the wonderful complexity of racial/ethnic and cultural diversity?

I have been so inspired by the work of psychologist Donald Winnicott, whose description of human development includes the ways a "good-enough" parent or caregiver creates an environment or container in which the baby/child grows.[4] Winnicott called that container in which development happens "transitional space." It is a space for play, creativity, imagination, and innovation. Psychiatrist and leadership theorist Ronald Heifetz pushed this psychological concept into the world of business, noting how our early ancestors' process of adaptation to new possibilities and challenges has continued over the course of written history, with the growth and variation in scope, structure, governance, strategy, and coordination of political and commercial enterprise.[5] The practice of managing these processes has also evolved; this management is what is called adaptive leadership. Adaptive leadership is the practice of wrestling with tough challenges through building on the past, experimenting, and gathering diverse perspectives in order for systems to thrive.

I believe effective leaders must create a container for adaptive learning, a space in which lessons are learned, new tools are developed, diversity is valued, and creativity takes place. Just like the child in Winnicott's theory develops in a good-enough container, leaders can create a good-enough container for experimentation, risk taking, failing, and innovating new strategies when they pay attention to cultivating community. Warm collegiality, celebrating wins, encouraging lessons from failures, straight talk and clear signals, gentle and private reprimands, play and joyfulness—these are some elements that make a container safe for adaptive learning.

Growing multicultural, multiracial communities inside the larger American community requires adaptive leadership and the creation of safe space for learning and development. It requires imagination, experimentation, diverse opinions, and creativity. Creating a container for adaptive learning is required to tackle tough problems like blending cultures while maintaining specificity or creating multiracial communities in the midst of a still-racist America. What does it look like to create such a container for adaptive learning? What does it mean to create a holding environment for the development of what the Rev. Dr. Martin Luther King Jr. would call the Beloved Community? How do we cultivate, care for, and nurture communities that thrive in their racial/ethnic and cultural diversity?

In my dissertation research, I was so fortunate to have deep conversations with five clergy and other leaders in their congregations. Let me introduce them:

Karen Sue Hernandez-Granzen is a "Newyorican" (Puerto Rican born in New York) Presbyterian clergyperson who proudly claims her Spanish, Taino Indian, and African Roots. At the time of the study, she had been the pastor of the Westminster Presbyterian Church—a 150-member community worshiping with 100—in Trenton, New Jersey, for nine years.

Randolph Cassells Charles, a white man who considers himself "ethnically Southern," had been the pastor of Epiphany Episcopal Church for nine years when we met. Growing up, he lived a relatively privileged life and knew few blacks, save his nanny. Epiphany, located in downtown Washington, D.C., is home to 150 homeless men, women, and children and another 150 diverse Episcopalians who gather for worship.

Jong Woo Park had been the pastor of Fairhaven United Methodist Church—the product of a merger of a northern white and a southern black church in the 1960s—in Gaithersburg, Maryland, for three years. J.W., as he is called, is a Korean man who was born in Seoul. Some two hundred people gather for worship each Sunday in two services, which blend traditions from the black church and mainline Methodist traditions.

Adrienne Brewington, an African-American woman, had been the pastor of Westbury United Methodist Church in Westbury, New York—a community of about 150 worshipers—for three years when I studied her congregation. She is the first woman and the first African American to serve this congregation in a community that has been biracial since the Quakers living there freed their slaves in the nineteenth century. Lay leaders are deeply committed to a vision of a racially and culturally diverse congregation.

Gordon Dragt, a white man born and raised in Michigan, had served as the senior minister of Middle Collegiate Church for nineteen years when we met. When he arrived, Middle Church had twenty-seven senior-age members; often the paid choir was larger than the worshiping community. Though he had been called to the congregation to close it, Gordon had a vision to create multiple portals of entry for people in the community. He knighted himself the pastor of "schmooze" and welcome, ushering diverse people into a radically welcoming space. Gordon made worship a joyful celebration, with classical and gospel music and arts of all kinds. (Gordon was a professional clown!) He also opened the doors for scores and scores of funerals for those dying from the HIV/AIDS epidemic.

In my research, I discovered five characteristics these leaders cultivated in thriving, multiracial, multicultural communities. First, these communities valued *radical truth telling and transparency*. Karen Hernandez-Granzen often said, *"No tengo pelos en la lengua* [I have no hair in my mouth]." This wonderful idiom means, "I will speak my mind." For Karen, speaking the truth in love was a guiding ethic for her congregation. She was fearless about "carefronting" the tough issues with firm love honed in truth. For her, this was one of the secrets to having a safe container in which people could test new ideas, try on new behaviors, be willing to fail, and try again to succeed. She recognized the vulnerability that people feel when in spaces that are unfamiliar, and her commitment was that truth would be a great equalizer, a tie that bound the community together.

Second, the communities valued a commitment to social justice as part of their identity. Randolph Charles was convinced that a commitment to eradicating poverty gave his congregation a transformational identity. Through his preaching and by his example, Randolph storied for his congregation their call to feed the poor and care for the homeless. Though they came from many cultures and stories, they were creating a new culture and a new story of altruism, kindness, and justice. They were creating a culture in which the power to heal the world surpassed anything that might divide them.

Third, the communities *embraced conflict* as part of their healthy thriving. Adrienne Brewington's community described her as a love agent who was fearless about conflict. She observed with a wide-open heart that being a multiracial, multicultural community is fraught with conflict. She encouraged expression of this conflict and regarded the creative energy it generated as a gift to the community. Her prayerful presence created a brave space for conflict to be expressed and addressed.

Fourth, these communities focused on what it means to *be on the border*. J.W. was Korean in an African American and white context. He created worship, education, and other programs that encouraged the congregation to take turns, to put themselves on the border of what the other generally enjoyed and wanted. Folk learned to live in the tension of the both/and (both white, black, and on the border), knowing that in time their favorite hymn would be sung in worship, their favorite food served in the fellowship hour. We'll talk more about what it means to be on the border in our chapter on communication.

Finally, hearing the stories of Gordon's leadership at Middle Church solidified my understanding the *power of story* to create a holding environment for the adaptive work of developing multiracial, multicultural communities. It is to this characteristic that I want to turn more fully. First, let me tell you about Howard Gardner's beautiful theory of story.

In a study of eleven leaders in his book *Leading Minds*, Gardner argues that the "ultimate impact of the leader depends most significantly on the particular story that he or she relates or embodies and the receptions to that story on the part of audiences (or collaborators or followers)."[6] In other words, leaders tell compelling stories that change the story: they help both leader and follower find their role in the unfolding story. Translating this to a faith perspective, I believe it is the task of adaptive leadership to help God's people understand the compelling story of God's amazing grace, love, and transformative power, and to help them find and own their role in healing souls and the world. Individuals and faith communities are formed by stories; they will be most transformed by stories that give meaning to their lives, stories that make sense, stories that fit "in terms of where they have been and where they would like to go."[7] Of course, the more familiar stories are the ones most well received; new stories encounter resistance. And stories delivered in more than one modality (you could consider it a form of glossolalia, or speaking in tongues) are the most pleasing and easy to incorporate into the life of the follower.

Though he was not familiar with this theory, Gordon Dragt was a consummate storyteller. Each Sunday during the eighteen months we worked together, I would marvel at the way Gordon used the announcements in worship to "story" his vision for the congregation. Announcement time was full of laughter, anecdotes, recognition of volunteers, and work well done. He'd move through the congregation, touching shoulders, storying all the time: "You are seen here, you are loved here, you belong here." Announcing "The sandwich-making program needs helpers" was not only a call to particular action but also a way to keep before the congregation, no matter which sermon was to follow, that Middle believes in hospitality, in feeding the poor, in making sure that everyone has enough.

Gordon retired in 2005, leaving me as senior minister of Middle Church. My staff and I are superaware of the power of stories. On Sundays, our announcements still story who we are. I invite visitors to stand, and we recognize visitors from Queens and Great Britain; from Paris and Park Slope, Brooklyn. We also recognize our growing online community.

Every year we invite people into structured storytelling. Sometimes we are doing this in one-on-one meetings. We might ask a congregant about how their spirits are. How is Middle Church working for them and their loved ones? What is something we could do better? Are you feeling called to any particular program or ministry? These one-hour conversations are rich in wisdom. But they also help the congregant feel seen, known, and loved. They feel connected in our community because their story matters.

Often we have these conversations in small groups. From our leadership council to our young adults, from our Moms-in-the-Middle to our choirs, we use existing groups and create focus groups to get people talking about their stories and sharing what they see for their own lives and for Middle Church. Here is an example of one such structured conversation. The Scriptures here are my canon, my go-to texts about love and justice. Of course, you can use texts that hold special meaning in your context.

STORYTELLING FOR SMALL GROUPS

1. Complete the sentence "For our church, 'I have a dream that someday . . .'"

2. Listen to these texts and ask, "What does this say about God's vision for the church?"

   Genesis 2:4–3:7   Amos 5:21–24
   Exodus 3:1–14   Isaiah 65:17–25
   Exodus 16:1–30   Luke 1:26–38

3. Which Bible story or image best speaks to the identity of our church, saying, "This is who we are"?

4. Imagine that the life of this church is an ongoing story. If you are writing this chapter in the story of this church, what is its title?

5. What is the title of the next chapter?

6. What will help write the next chapter and what will hinder it?

7. If values are defined as the way we do what we do, make a list of the values you see lived out in this church; explain how they are expressed in behaviors. In other words, what are the norms by which we live out our values?

8. If a vision is a picture of a preferred reality, what is your vision for this congregation? In other words, what is God calling us to do, in such a time as this?

9. What do we need in order to fulfill this call, in terms of resources? Money? Staff? Volunteers? Space?

10. What will *you* do in order to fulfill God's call on our lives?

Here are other ways we use the power of story to cultivate a communal container for the important work of building a multiracial, multicultural community in which racial/ethnic and cultural diversity is not just tolerated but is also celebrated as our highest value.

- At the beginning of every consistory meeting (the fancy name for our board of directors), we check in over supper together. I offer a question to help frame our sharing, something generic enough that allows space for innovation. All board members share in turn what they are celebrating and their current struggles. Then we pray. We know that together we are weaving a new story and that it is articulated through our individual stories.
- We invite people to *join the movement* we call Middle Church six times a year. The first hour of the gathering of those who are coming to be part of our community is time to share their spiritual journeys. We ask, "What is your spiritual journey, and how did it bring you to Middle Church?" Those stories stick with people, helping them find connections with one another in this new community. Our recent addition is a twice-a-year retreat for new(ish) members so they can grow deeper roots, find their own ministries at Middle Church, and not slip out the back door.
- With our learning groups—our Healing Racism Task Force or our Young Adult Leadership Lab, for example—we might invite a structured conversation in a super-mini retreat, where the only agenda is sharing stories. For that, we use the questions we shared with you in the vision process in chapter 2, "Casting the Vision," and ask, "What Is Your Story?" (see above). Here is how it goes:

What Is Your Story? A Super-Mini Retreat
- Allow 2.5 hours for this process. Provide copies of questions, or post them on chart paper for all to use. It would be helpful to provide snacks and beverages; breaking bread together builds community.
- Invite people to find a partner and to use questions 1–3 to share with each other. Instruct the pairs to make eye contact, holding the space with attention to listening rather than planning to speak, and invite them to share the time equally. Allow thirty minutes for this exercise.
- When the pair finishes sharing, invite them to find another pair and to share on questions 4–6. Encourage them to choose a pair that will increase the diversity of perspectives in the conversation. Allow forty-five minutes for this.
- Allow for a fifteen-minute break, and then invite the groups of four to find another group of four and finish with the remaining four questions, allowing sixty minutes for this conversation.
- Invite the group to close with a prayer, each person saying a sentence.

In conclusion, cultivating a community means knowing each other, celebrating each other, having empathy for one another, supporting one another. This work can begin with storytelling in one-on-one conversations and in small groups. Conversations and storytelling help to cultivate shared vision, theology, and ethics. They are the bedrock for the emerging community. Storytelling is one powerful way to create a container in which the adaptive work of thriving in a multiracial, multicultural context can happen. And not only that; it is also the way Middle Church has deepened its work and moved along a continuum from celebrating diversity to actively working against racism.

Every leader in a multiracial, multicultural faith community is coauthoring a new group story, one that frankly goes against the grain of a too-often-segregated America, and a group sense of call informed by the stories of the leaders, by members' stories and master stories (for example, the biblical narratives, and binding narratives, like being chosen). The stories we tell are inevitably shaped by our own, so knowing ourselves fully is such an important capacity. A good spiritual director, therapist, or even a best friend can help us stay in touch with our own stories. Our self-awareness puts us more in tune with the fears, hopes, dreams, and insecurities imbedded in the stories we hear. This increases our emotional intelligence and our ability to hold the racial/ethnic and cultural diversity of our contexts. Stories shared in worship, in rituals, in liturgy, even in potluck suppers build trust, create and uncover shared values, and bind the community together.

Review Stage 2 of the Pentecost Paradigm

– Is the congregation deep into storytelling?

_____

_____

_____

_____

_____

_____

– Are they sharing with each other the messages they received about race while growing up?

_____

_____

_____

_____

_____

– Have your leaders agreed to read and discuss a relevant book together? View a film?

_____

_____

_____

_____

_____

Chapter 7

Celebrating in Worship

*W*hen I (Jacqui) was a little girl memorizing the Lord's Prayer, I struggled with phrases like "Hallowed be thy name." My brain heard "How low wet" and could not understand what that had to do with God! But "on earth as it is in heaven," I got that. Even as my notions of heaven have turned away from streets paved with gold and pearly gates, I am deeply inspired by the concept that whatever good might be in heaven can be here on earth, today, right now. This passage from John's Revelation describes more fully for me what that means:

> See, the home of God is among mortals.
> He will dwell with them; they will be his peoples,
> and God himself will be with them;
> he will wipe every tear from their eyes.
> Death will be no more;
> mourning and crying and pain will be no more,
> for the first things have passed away.
> (Revelation 21:3–5)

This vision of God living among and within human beings—comforting, healing, and making all things new—inspires our community at Middle Collegiate Church to lean into the world as it can be. It empowers us to actively participate in the healing of the world.

Defining Worship

What exactly is worship? The word "worship" comes from Old English *weorthscipe*, meaning "worthiness" or "respect." *Webster's Dictionary* says that worship is "reverence offered a divine being or supernatural power; also, an act of expressing such reverence or a form of religious practice with its creed and ritual." According to Thayer's Greek Lexicon, the Greek word that translates into *worship* is *proskyneō*, which means to "kiss the hand to (toward) one, in token of reverence; to fall upon the knees and touch the ground with the forehead as an expression of profound reverence by kneeling or prostration to do homage (to one) or make obeisance, whether in order to express respect or to make supplication." The Hebrew word is *shachah*, which means "to bow down, or pay homage."

All this sounds as though worship is about giving honor to God, bowing down to God, revering God. But worship gives us something as well. We believe that worship is the transformational moment that engages us in the recognition of the power of God at work in and through us. In other words, worship rehearses the reign of God on earth. In worship, the

Creator God is present, Christ is present, and the Holy Spirit is present. God is there in worship, scripting our lives for service, writing the dream of God's shalom on our hearts, participating in our transformation such that we might transform the world. Our minds are renewed, our vision is made clear; through the preached word, the sharing of sacraments, in music, prayers, and art—God's intention becomes ours. As the worship team and I plan worship, we imagine that our offering is lavish love poured out for God, in homage to God, who is the object of our affection. God is the audience for our worship, but God is also acting in worship, participating and performing in worship, alongside the preacher, the choirs, and the liturgists. We believe all of the people are liturgists, the ones in the pews and the ones at the pulpit. In other words, God is audience and actor; so are those gathered also audience and actors. All are performing the preferred vision; all are rehearsing the reign of God. Worship stories who we are, as the people of God. It shapes our stories.

Plan with Intention

Although my official (and old-fashioned!) title at Middle Church is Senior Minister-in-Charge, my working title is Minister for Vision, Worship/Arts, and Public Theology. Worship generates public theology; it turns people on to imagine the world that God desires. With that in mind, everything that happens in worship, from beginning to end, helps create God-talk that is transformational.

Our intention is to plan worship one year in advance, with space to drop in details as we move through the year. We ask ourselves, "What is God calling us to story this year in worship? What themes will we use, and how will the Lectionary passages help us to support those themes?"

For example, my staff and I decided that our theme for program year 2017–18 (July 1, 2017—June 30, 2018) would be "Complete the Dream." The double entendre was intentional: we felt that the world was calling us to complete God's dream; also, recognizing the fiftieth anniversary of the assassination of the Rev. Dr. Martin Luther King Jr. (in 1968), we felt compelled to work with other congregations to complete his dream as well. Our Vision 2020 ministry plan called us to work as follows:

1. For racial reconciliation and healing the scars of white supremacy;
2. For economic justice, including a living wage, affordable housing, and raising the future of poor children through education in after-school and summer programs;
3. Against mass incarceration, militarization, and the cradle-to-prison pipeline;
4. For LGBTQ justice, with an emphasis on transgender rights, countering the particular danger to trans-people of color;
5. For gender justice, including equal pay and a woman's right to choose; against global discrimination and wage disparity.

Our ministry plan guides not only programs and budget but also our preaching and worship plans. We are intentional, then, about the theme "Complete the Dream" and the way we story our partnership with God in worship.

Our Intention Is Our Sermon

Just as we are intentional about our theme and the story we hope to tell, we are also intentional about who we "cast" in worship and what role each person plays every Sunday. Who is at the pulpit, preaching, praying, and leading worship? Which lay leader or family is reading Scripture or offering the invitation to join our movement? We are particular even in the language we use about membership and to invite our offering; for example, "Join the movement" means to become part of the body of Christ at Middle Church *and* it means give of yourself, your time, and your financial resources to power the movement with love.

Who greets at the door? How do they welcome those who are gathering? What do worshipers see first when they arrive? What is the story being told in the bulletin? How do hymns and musical selections offer a radical welcome to a diverse group of people? How are we responding to the children in our midst? How do we ask for the offering and invite people to join us? Since it is our intention to be multiracial and multicultural, each one of these decisions about people leading worship furthers our intention. When people come to worship, whether for the first time or the hundredth time, the unspoken sermon is whom they observe in leadership. We ask these questions when we plan worship because the entire worship celebration tells the story of who God is and how we help God to heal the world.

Unity in Diversity

While our staff represents diverse theological perspectives—some of us more traditionally Christian and others more Universalist in our understanding of God's redemptive work in the world—we are deeply committed to using inclusive language in worship. When it makes sense, we use no pronouns for God, and when we do use pronouns, we alternate "he" and "she." We are also inclusive in speaking theologically about God's love shown in Jesus Christ as a wide-open door, not a litmus test that God's people can fail. Though we are Christian, we understand that God speaks many languages. We take care not to leave our non-Christian family (yes, we have Jewish members, some humanists, and one Muslim member) outside of the grace we believe God is offering to us in worship. The way we think and talk about the God we worship reflects our intention to be in interreligious, interfaith partnerships as we seek to repair the world. We regard the faith-walk of those around us with respect and care.

Music Matters

At Middle Church, we express our yearning to be in the center of God's plan for healing our souls and healing the world in our music and in the arts. Once a theme has been decided upon for a season of worship, the minister who is preaching selects a text—usually one from the Revised Common Lectionary—and shares the text, a sermon title, and a few sentences expressing what the sermon promises to do. With this summary, the music and worship team and I begin our work to think of creative ways to express our yearning to be part of God's plan for humanity in worship and the arts for this particular sermon as well as for the worship arc of the year. We choose music from all eras of traditional Western church music, from the cultures that may be particularly appropriate for our congregation, and from cultures that may have interesting and evocative traditions. We include music from Broadway shows, which may fit a specific theme. All styles, in other words, are welcome. We also consider not only the liturgical calendar but also secular calendars, noting things like World AIDS Day; African American, Asian American, or Latinx History Months; Women's History Month; Labor Day; Native American Day; Memorial Day; Pride Month; Independence Day; and Juneteenth. In every way that we can imagine, worship helps to create the story we are sure God is writing with humankind. For example, on the Sunday before Columbus Day and at Thanksgiving, we commemorate Native American people and their contributions. We do this because we know that Christopher Columbus did not discover America but rather happened upon a land that was already inhabited

At Middle Church we now have five choirs. Here in New York City, it is quite common to have a paid, professional choir in houses of worship. With so many musicians seeking work, a weekly choir position is prized. Our Middle Church Choir is twelve paid singers. Three singers for each of four parts, they are amazingly gifted sight readers who rehearse for ninety minutes before worship and then stun us with the music they offer. Our choir is world class; many of them perform on Broadway and in classical concerts all around the country. They sing everything from Bach to the Beatles to Irving Berlin. They sing jazz, spirituals, and anthems with such beauty. I have colleagues who tell me they don't worship when at church because they are working. I like to sit right up front when the Middle Church Choir is singing; I can hear them breathe and feel the power of their voices flowing over me. It makes me a better preacher; they help me worship!

The In-the-Middle Chorus sings about once a month and every Sunday in the summer. They are volunteers who have a more classical taste and are supported by four paid section leaders. Our music team is working to get more people singing more genres of music; this is all part of our call to create space for our racial/ethnic and cultural diversity as we worship.

Our Middle Community Chorus was called into being by Emmy-nominated actor and singer Tituss Burgess (*The Unbreakable Kimmy Schmidt*). In this chorus are the artists who launched our Art & Soul Sunday night worship celebrations, and they sing for special occasions. They are young adults, many of them Tituss's students, who sing on Broadway and are aspiring to television careers. They are featured on the Middle Church album *Welcome!*, was recorded by Tituss. (You can find that album on our Web site at middlechurch.org and at iTunes. All of the proceeds from sales fund our justice ministries.)

The Village Chorus for Children and Youth sings once a month. It is remarkable that our youngest singers have just learned to read and our oldest singers are in high school. They are learning, through the music, about the power of song to change hearts and minds. They also help us mark Children's Sabbath, Christmas, and Children's Day in June, offering music from the movement, Broadway shows, and the world.

The Jerriese Johnson Gospel Choir is named for its founder, a charismatic African-American actor who found his way to Middle Church in the late 1970s. A tall man with a big heart, Jerriese became an important part of the redeveloping church, serving on the consistory and helping my predecessor, Gordon Dragt, figure out how to grow membership. Jerriese asked to start a community gospel choir, one in which you could drop in and sing without signing up to join the church. He shared Gordon's "just as you are as you come through the door" welcoming spirit. At first the choir was small and mighty, sort of like Jerriese Johnson and the Pips! But soon word spread in the East Village that Middle Church was a place where you could come, be loved, hear a meaningful sermon and music from two choirs, and then you'd walk out ready for the week. Now our all-volunteer gospel choir is some forty singers strong—a rainbow of diversity; they are black, white, Latino, and Asian; old and young; gay and straight. They are representative of the racial/ethnic and cultural diversity of Middle Church. And they can sing! Some are professionals; most grew up singing in chorus. All of them give up two hours each Thursday night to learn music and pray with each other. They are our largest "small group."

One April, at our annual conference for leaders in multiracial, multicultural congregations, our Gospel Choir sang the Academy Award–winning song "Glory," penned by John Legend and Common, featured in the movie *Selma*. Alex, a tall, black gay man with a beautiful tenor voice, sang the lead with such passion. And the choir "rapped" the special piece, in unison, all dressed in black and white. The congregation was on its feet! By the end, we all were singing, "One day, when the glory comes it will be ours. . . ."[1]

Arts in Worship

At Middle Church, we believe the arts represent several cultural languages to use in worship. The arts speak directly to the heart. In our worship planning meetings, we dream of ways to punctuate the themes we are storying with art.

One Easter morning we put a tarp on the floor near the pulpit. One of our visual artists, Mary Jo, came to church dressed in coveralls, with her oils, brushes, and a vision to paint worship. Beginning with the prelude, she painted the introit, the prayers, the hymns, and the sermon. We watched as her blank white canvas turned into a cacophony of color. She painted the awe of the spirit we all felt. If your space doesn't lend itself to indoor painting, imagine taking worship outside in the streets, displaying beautifully painted panels while marching for justice. Or create a graffiti wall where neighborhood youth are invited to paint their vision of God.

Frog and Toad were favorite puppet characters of my friend Gordon Dragt. They made many appearances at Middle Church during Gordon's tenure. In their earliest iterations, two actors performed Frog and Toad behind a puppet theater. Now, with the advent of the Broadway performances of *Avenue Q* and *Hand to God*, in which puppeteers are fully visible to the audience, we find it delightful to see our actors with their arms in the puppets. It gives us a chance to celebrate Frog and Toad, along with Elisabeth and Dean, who play them. Frog and Toad have taken on serious issues like bullying and gay bashing. They have prayed in worship and have led songs. They have invited people to join the church!

Besides music, dance is the art we use most. Black shoes have tapped in our choir loft. Modern dancers have draped their bodies on our pews. Ballet dancers have balanced delicately on the pulpit chair. We have many choreographers in our community. Some have their own companies, like Kim Grier at Rod Rodgers Dance. Mark Dendy choreographs large pieces of work all over the nation. We have dancers from Alvin Ailey, Martha Graham, Garth Fagan and The Dance Theater of Harlem. They are as diverse as my taste in dance. Ishmael Houston-Jones throws his body around in loose movements that seem unchoreographed but are intricate works of art. Adrienne and Lutin are a couple who bring different schools of dance to shared pieces that they both choreograph and perform. Some of our dancers are actors who can dance, folks who used to dance, yoga folk who move a little, and some like me who took dance as a child and love to shake it to R&B (rhythm and blues). Some bring cultural and national (Japanese, Chinese) forms with them to the sanctuary.

With this diverse collection of dancers and choreographers, we have surprised the congregation with dancers rising up out of the pews, climbing to the tops of them, dancing in pairs down the aisles. We have danced with a large silk blue "river" on Earth Day. A couple and their children have danced to Michael Jackson's "Man in the Mirror." We have enjoyed voguing on the pulpit as part of our celebration of Pride Month and Ballroom culture. And yes, classical ballet happens too!

We are blessed with this diversity in New York City. In your context, you might invite a step-team from a local high school, a graduating class from a local dance studio, or a dance major at a local university to offer their gifts in your congregation in exchange for rehearsal space.

Celebrating Ethnicity Grows Diversity

When I came to Middle Church in 2004, I was stunned at the racial/ethnic diversity. We were mostly white, with a nice-sized community of African-American members. There were about ten Latinx and two or three Chinese members. One of them was a spunky, smart woman named Gloria; anytime we were naming our diversity, "We are Black, White, Latino . . . ," and before we could finish, she railed, "Don't forget *Asian*!" Her critique led to a one-on-one conversation and a plan to celebrate Lunar New Year.

I worked with Gloria, my staff, and our music team to create a Lunar New Year celebration that would work in our context. We thought it should be nontraditional, Pan-Asian, to celebrate the Japanese, Chinese, Korean, and Indian members of our congregation.

Gloria and Jocelyn, a lovely author who has a Chinese father and a white mother, wrote prayers. Chad, who grew up in Hawaii of Japanese and Korean parents, preached. A group of Japanese women who sing in our gospel choir sang special music in Japanese and in English. We invited a koto player to join us. Kashimi danced the Fan Dance. Gloria passed out red envelopes so we could take up a special offering for survivors of an earthquake in Japan.

The church was so excited to have this new kind of celebration in our midst. Four Japanese women, led by Kaede, and one African-American soprano, Tina, formed the group Rising Sun! Now they sing every Lunar New Year celebration, which always occurs in February, when we are celebrating African-American History Month. As we have continued this tradition, our gospel choir has more Asian diversity—Japanese, Chinese, and Vietnamese. The Salim family has grown, marrying and having children who are baptized in our midst. The Wu family—mom, dad, and three children, who found us by way of an organist friend—have grown up at Middle Church. The Wu children sing in the choir, make sandwiches for our feeding ministry, and James, their dad, is an elder on our board. Every year, more and more, our gospel choir looks like the United Nations!

In 2017 we not only celebrated Lunar New Year; we also celebrated Pan Asian American History month in May. On one May Sunday, a hundred judges and court officers from Judicial Friends, a traditionally African-American and Latinx group of judges, joined us for worship. What a remarkable day. One hundred esteemed guests in black robes processed behind our two choirs. Kashimi danced a beautiful piece she had choreographed when a tsunami hit Japan. And the growing-up Wu children offered a prayer with their dad. The multicultural, multiracial identity of Middle Church was in full regalia, as colorful as Kashimi's scarf.

Because we are who we are, our Latinx family yearned for more celebration of the unique cultures that they represent. And so it is that now we use two Sundays in September/October to celebrate the many cultures of our Latinx/Hispanic family. Worship, my sermon in Spanglish, education programs, and food from several Latinx cultures after worship teach Middle Church *que somos Latinos también* (that we are Latinx too). In solidarity with our Puerto Rican family, we are engaged in ongoing recovery and repair work necessitated by Hurricane Maria.

From King Day to Hoodies

I preached my first sermon at Middle Church as a guest preacher on Martin Luther King Sunday in 2003. Gordon Dragt was as deeply impacted as I was by the murder of Dr. King. Every January, he invited a guest preacher to celebrate King Day; I was honored to have the chance. When I joined the staff in January 2004, I suggested that we celebrate not just one Sunday but a month of Sundays in February to honor Black History Month. This tradition was met with great appreciation by almost all of the congregation. We sang gospel hymns and spirituals. Jazz music was accompanied by tap and modern dance. Our entire congregation became students of W. E. B. Du Bois, James Baldwin, Howard Thurman, Alice Walker, and Toni Morrison as they showed up in sermons. One sermon was pulled straight from the mouth of Baby Suggs, holy, and her speech in the clearing of Morrison's book *Beloved*.

I had been at Middle for eight years when Trayvon Martin was killed on February 26, 2012. The murder of this young boy devastated us. I remember driving with my husband the evening Trayvon was killed, and John said, "Middle has to do something. We always do something."

"I know," I replied. "Do you have any ideas?"

John said, "What if we wear hoodies, in solidarity with Trayvon?"

I immediately called our media and outreach team. This was on a Friday evening. They put out a call via our social media and created a special e-letter to say that we would all wear hoodies on Sunday in worship. Further, we asked that folks would bring extra ones if they could, to share with those who were without hoodies.

I arrived on Sunday to discover that even my classically trained director of music had purchased a hoodie from Abercrombie & Fitch! Hoodies in the choir loft, hoodies in every pew—we were in uniform, in our diversity, in solidarity with a boy who seemed dangerous because of his hoodie. Pictures of Middle Church members in our hoodies appeared in the *Washington Post* and the *New York Times*, and on MSNBC and CNN. One of our members wrote a song in honor of Trayvon, and our gospel choir learned and sang it. Trayvon's life gave us the opportunity to live out a new dimension of our identity. Not only were we intentionally multiracial and multicultural; not only did we celebrate diversity as part of God's rich creation; we also understood that we were called to be *antiracist* as part of our life of faith.

Standing up for Trayvon meant standing up for our values. It meant standing up for the rights of black people to live free of racism. When Michael Brown was killed, we prayed with our hands up, once again in solidarity, with the uprising in Ferguson (2014) and the young people who took to the streets to say enough is enough.

I was on vacation when Michael Brown was killed, and our staff did an excellent job of organizing our congregation that August. When I returned in September, I found myself drawn into a movement for racial justice with colleagues all over the globe. We used the Internet to teach and organize. Outraged by the chokehold killing of Eric Garner and the nonindictment of the police officer who killed him and haunted by his "I can't breathe . . . ," we could hardly catch our breath. Our nation was on fire over what seemed to be state-sanctioned killings of black people. Sandy Bland, Arlington Sterling—the list is so long. We marched and we "died-in" on the streets of New York, in our sanctuary, and in a cafeteria full of Washington electeds in our nation's capital. My preaching and teaching were calls for justice.

One Sunday morning I preached a sermon about my niece, Rio, and her innocent view of the world. That was the Sunday that a little girl named Diamond had watched from the backseat of the car as the man who raised her was shot to death by a policeman. By putting together the stories of Rio and Diamond—two four-year-old little girls—I was able to take Middle Church further on our journey toward racial justice work.

What I know to be true is this: worship is one of the most powerful tools for community organizing available to a congregation. Music, art, preaching, and prayers can transform hearts and minds; it can story for them the role God has commissioned for the individual and congregation in healing the world. Because the work of multiracial, multicultural life in an ongoing context of segregation, racism, and xenophobia is difficult, and because worship that calls for this difficult work might engender conflict, congregational leaders need courage in order to lead their congregations into this transformational work.

Worship creates a container, a holy space for listening to what God requires of us, as articulated in Scripture, in prayers, in the preached word. Music and the arts drop us right into the vision that God has for us. Each week at Middle Church, adult education in the form of a sermon talkback (response) helps the word to keep becoming flesh. The preacher of the day also puts things to do in the bulletin each week—some that focus on interior work and other tasks that are about learning or living the transformation being preached. Both the talkback and tasks are designed to echo and amplify the call on our lives to do justice, love kindness, and walk humbly with our God (cf. Micah 6:8). God's dream is our dream, and worship keeps this before God's people.

In summary, worship helps us perceive the new thing that God is doing as we celebrate the worthiness of our God. In and through worship, we rehearse the reign of God on earth, as it is in heaven. Worship heals our souls so we can heal the world. It is also the space where we share the Sacred Narrative and cast ourselves in it. How can we discover it? What is our role in it? The Sacred Narrative *contradicts and critiques* our current story. This means that worship is both a celebration *and* a call to change! Worship is the place where the sense of urgency for the new story is created and also nurtured in "safe-enough" or brave space. Because we want everyone to get it, we need to tell that story in the many cultural languages of our people. We need to be multivocal in our worship planning so that as many as are able will find their place in the purpose of the Holy.

We will *not* grow multiracial and multicultural communities with unimaginative worship that represents only one culture. Our musicians, clergy staff, and lay artists have to share our vision for racial/ethnic and cultural diversity and also have capacities to enact it. Worship needs to address the living texts of congregants, who are moving in a complex world. Time for mourning happens in prayer; time for activism happens when we wear hoodies in solidarity, or take worship to the street in the Pride March each year. Worship puts our living texts, the cultural texts, and the Sacred Narrative in conversation, making meaning of lives, culture, and world—and transforming them all.

As a consultant to congregations, John has worshiped in churches of every size and cultural setting across numerous denominational traditions. I agree with John that every faith community has its own personality, its own culture. The culture is shaped by norms and beliefs that are both articulated and unarticulated, conscious and unconscious, based on long-practiced faith traditions and based on contemporary and even secular customs and preferences. Congregational culture includes how they worship. Some have expansive liturgy, some have minimal liturgy, and some have no liturgy at all. Each worship form says something about the congregation's history, core values, identity, and culture.

John tells a story of attending a particular Korean church for worship. He says, "I could feel the energy of the children, notice the eye contact from adults who nodded to me and smiled a greeting, and see the friendliness of the people toward each other. I experienced the culture without knowing the language. I took a seat by myself and almost immediately noticed someone taking a seat next to me. As I turned to see who it was, it was a man who asked me in English if I spoke Korean. When I said, "No, I do not," he replied, "I will be your translator during the worship celebration." This and many other experiences in worship settings led me to ask: Do the members of the congregation determine the form, spirit, and culture of worship? Or does the worship experience shape the culture of the congregation? We believe both are true. Below are helpful tips for planning worship to increase the racial/ethnic and cultural diversity in your context.

Worshiping Our Way to Diversity
- Select themes and plan worship for the whole year, working far in advance to create a frame into which you can drop details. Planning makes space for art to happen. Be prepared to shift your plan for a changing environment. See the Reproducible Worship Planning Worksheet below.
- Invite people in your congregation and surrounding community, including children, to offer art in worship. Their presence immediately increases your diversity, and they will invite friends to come! Community colleges have affordable art to offer.
- Plan to preach texts that paint a picture of God's peaceable reign, such as Isaiah 11 and Revelation 7. Use illustrations and stories from many cultures in your sermons. Google is our friend. When writing, I might search "Latino man saves African American boy" and see what comes up.
- Start a gospel choir, no matter the racial or ethnic mix in your congregation. The local high school has some Glee-type teens who are ready to help you start an intergenerational choir.
- Secular music like jazz, R&B, classical, rock, and rap can help to build cultural bridges. For example, Michael Jackson's "Man in the Mirror" is a secular song with spiritual meaning. Music draws diverse people together in the world and does the same within our congregations.
- Hire a musician who is complementary to your style, one who shares your vision for racial and cultural diversity. Collaborate and celebrate the product in worship.
- Use cultural markers such as Black History Month, Lunar New Year, and Hispanic Heritage Month as opportunities to plan worship that celebrates a particular culture and invites others to "play" in it.

Use the planning document below to develop the multicultural, multiracial story you tell through worship.

A WORKSHEET FOR PLANNING MULTIRACIAL, MULTICULTURAL WORSHIP

Date	*Date and any special holidays or observances for this day*
Preacher(s)	
Scripture(s)	
Sermon title/focus	*What is the title of the sermon? Write a sentence or two describing what the sermon will say and do.*
Theme	*What is the story we are telling right now? What is the theme for this liturgical arc?*
Leaders	*All lay and clergy leaders in worship. Assign their roles in the spaces below. Think diversity.*
	Announcements:
	Song leader:
	Scripture reader:
	First prayer:
	Second prayer:
	Offertory prayer:
	Communion servers:
Hymns/congregational singing	*Consider ALL the music—hymns, choir selections, special music, and so forth—as you make your plan. Do the selections for the week express our diverse, multivocal community? Can we make different choices to reach more hearts and souls?*

Choirs and/or other special music	Introit:
	Anthem:
	Offertory:
	Other:
Special art/event	*How can we use a variety of art to enhance and punctuate the message? Dance? Drama? Puppets? Visual? Can the sermon be a poem? Benediction a song? Can the dancers "move" to the Scripture? How can we make the art happen in a liturgical spot so we can keep our time commitment to the congregation?*
Sound/microphones	*Who is on which mic so that sound enhances rather than distracts from worship?*
Staging	*Who is in the pulpit? Where will we position the piano? How will we do Communion this month? We are ALWAYS painting a picture of the multiracial, multicultural vision.*
Notes	*Is there anything we need to consider about liturgy, for example, the Lord's Supper or baptism? Renewal of baptismal vows or new members joining? What accessibility? Ability? Content? Length of worship? An extra hymn?*
Resources	*Besides favorites such as* Prepare! A Weekly Worship Planbook for Pastors and Musicians *and hymnals such as* New Century, Presbyterian, Methodist, Rejoice in the Lord, African American, *and* Songs of Zion, *we look for resources from many faith traditions and cultures. We consider songs from the Broadway corpus and from popular music. We also flip through the index of music that resides in our heads. Secular songs become sacred here.*

Review Stage 2 and 3 of the Pentecost Paradigm

– What new elements have begun to be introduced into worship?

_____

_____

_____

– Are sermons setting forth God's vision for a multiracial, multicultural world?

_____

_____

– Are there intentional ways the congregation is being "held," sharing in educational events, and deepening awareness of justice issues?

_____

_____

– Have changes occurred in how the congregation provides welcome and hospitality?

_____

_____

– Who are the partners you have identified and are cultivating?

_____

_____

– Are there regular opportunities for the congregation to gather in dialogue to rehearse God's call and the congregation's commitment to becoming an inclusive faith community?

_____

_____

_____

Chapter 8

Understanding Congregational Conflict

A good friend of mine once observed, "Where two or three are gathered together, there will be conflict." Conflict in faith communities is both normative and, when healthy, can lead to creativity and new possibilities, but it is also potentially ruinous, leading to systems paralysis, congregational spats, and wounded people left cynical about religious institutions altogether. "If the church can't resolve its differences in the spirit of love, what hope is there for the rest of the world?" was one of the parting observations made by a congregational leader while leaving the church and leaving behind all religious practice. Leaders must have the ability to manage conflict in congregational life or they will become party to its destructive outcomes. Avoidance is rarely the best strategy.

Conflict can be rooted in any of several sources, and more than one source may be at play at any one time. It is helpful to know what is happening below the surface as well as what is observable in a conflict situation. It is a trait of emotional intelligence that we can identify what is happening underneath the observable feelings of anger and defensiveness and the behaviors of threat, accusation, or withdrawal. Here are some common sources of conflict:

1. *Core values.* When our core values are questioned or challenged, it can register as an assault on our personhood or even our worldview. In some congregations, conflicting core values about the presence of young children in worship has been a point of significant difference.
2. *Basic beliefs and theological differences.* How we perceive God and what we focus on in the biblical text can become fault lines in the faith community and determine who is "in" and who is "out," who is welcome and who is not.
3. *Worship forms and rituals.* Changes in orders of worship, worship styles, and hymn selection can become serious breaches of tradition and expectation.
4. *Power and control.* In many congregations, members will defer to matriarchs or patriarchs to determine decisions. When this becomes the unspoken norm and is accidentally or intentionally transgressed, conflict is sure to follow.
5. *Interpersonal issues.* Leadership styles or behavior patterns such as manipulation, bullying, or long-standing personal feuds can tear congregations apart.
6. *Intrapersonal issues.* Unresolved personal issues, a lack of self-awareness, or a tendency to view others with suspicion can play havoc in community life.
7. *Secular business norms.* Some lay leaders can become frustrated if they apply corporate-world administrative styles to faith community norms, where the processes may be as important as the outcomes and volunteers are not seen as employees.
8. *Unresolved grief, secrets, and boundary issues.* When past events in the story of the congregation are buried and unacknowledged, they can resurface to be relitigated and attached to a current circumstance.

71

9. *Institutional issues.* Polity constraints, differing priorities, and allocation of resources are examples of tensions in the system that can divide the energies of the community.
10. *Social issues.* Congregations often avoid becoming publically engaged on controversial issues in the interest of congregational peace. However, when convictions solidify on a particular issue, it can threaten a sense of harmony in the congregation and even bring about a split in the church.

There can be compounding and contributing factors to these sources. One such factor is that hurtful behaviors exhibited in response to the presenting issue can become the central issue. When civility and grace are abandoned in the process of an exchange of views, such behaviors can result in irreparable damage in the faith community. Additionally, when communication becomes guarded and anxiety-driven, or there is a lack of transparency or withholding of information, or a choosing of sides—then tensions and suspicions can arise and result in a hypersensitive climate in the system. When these factors are adjudicated on social media, it is done to the utter detriment of the faith community. Living in a culture as we do, of incivility and invective, it is helpful for the congregation to develop a "behavioral covenant," a set of norms for how the congregation will be in community together as a matter of spiritual practice. The following is one example of a congregational covenant:

A Congregational Covenant

1. *Foster a caring community*: We will act with kindness, empathy, and compassion.
2. *Celebrate our differences*: We will set aside our individual agendas and look for common ground so as to find the "we" in our journey together.
3. *Encourage trust and respect*: We will nurture a safe and supportive atmosphere, respectfully address concerns, seek productive resolution of conflict when it arises, and help others in that process.
4. *Support our community and leadership*: We will participate in and provide support to our community as well as our committees and leaders. We will share the work of advancing our congregational vision and goals.

Speed Leas, widely known for his expertise in congregational dynamics, identifies five levels of conflict that may occur in congregational life. These levels, while suggesting a progression in the severity of conflict, assume that conflict is always present in any human system.[1]

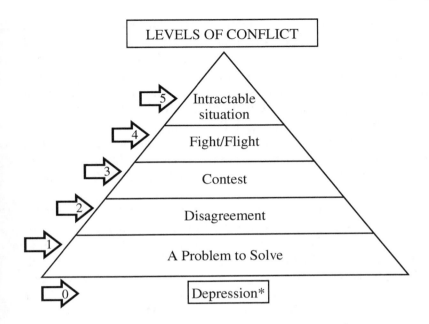

Levels of Conflict

Level One: A Problem to Solve
Conflicting goals, values, needs. Problem oriented rather than person oriented.

Level Two: Disagreement
Mixing of personalities and issues, problem cannot be clearly defined. Beginning of distrust and personalizing problem.

Level Three: Contest
Begin the dynamics of "win/lose." Personal attacks. Formation of factions, sides, camps. Distortion of information is a major problem.

Level Four: Fight/Flight
Shifts from winning to getting rid of person(s). Factions are solidified. Talk now takes on the language of "principles," not "issues."

Level Five: Intractable Situations
No longer clear understanding of issue(s); personalities have become the focus. Conflict is now unmanageable. Energy is centered on the elimination and/or destruction of the person(s).

Level Zero: Depression
Depression is defined as "anger turned inward." Sometimes congregations do not know they are in conflict because they are in a state of depression and denial. The task is to raise their awareness that there are problems to be solved. A congregation in depression exhibits low affect and low energy.

In multicultural, multiracial faith communities, sometimes issues of race and gender will be avoided to ensure congregational harmony. We simply don't talk about it. We avoid being accused of bias or racism or of being too "politically correct" or of being an angry person of color. It is likely that in such faith communities unintended racial and cultural offenses generating hurt feelings, frustration, and anger will accumulate over time when not discussed openly. When this happens, people will either quietly disappear or challenge congregational "harmony" by expressing how they feel, but doing so in unhelpful ways. A congregation cannot be truly diverse and inclusive by not talking about the most sensitive issues of race and gender. Such conversations must be ongoing and be firmly woven into the life of the congregation. Structured conversations in a safe setting can be educational, healing, and freeing.

In the case of Middle Church, great care and intentionality is practiced to facilitate these conversations. The staff invited a diverse group of participants to commit to a yearlong process of study, conversation, and healing focused on white supremacy, racial bias, and racism. The gatherings included viewings of *RIKERS: An American Jail*, a documentary by Bill Moyers; *I Am Not Your Negro*, based on the words of James Baldwin; and Ava DuVernay's documentary *13th*. Together we read James Baldwin's *The Fire Next Time*, which is a letter to his nephew; and Ta-Nehisi Coates's book *Between the World and Me*, a letter to his son. Members of the group were then asked to write their own letter to someone important to them, expressing their thoughts, hopes, and experiences regarding race. These letters may become a booklet for the congregation and others.

Additionally, four or five group members of the same ethnicity were invited into a "fishbowl" to sit together in the center of the room while Task Force members encircled them. Those identifying as African American came to the center of the room to respond to the question "What do you say about race when people of another ethnicity are not around?" In turn, both a group identifying more generally as "persons of color" and a white group sat in the center to discuss the same question. This experience was profound for many of us. It was the conversation we rarely hear from one another.

Such structured conversations can be held once the group has developed a sense of trust and all have agreed to a shared set of norms for how the learning community will do its work. Also, there were skilled facilitators in the room. In this setting true feelings can be expressed and experiences shared. Some hard things were talked about that day that deepened intimacy and pulled the curtain back on the challenges we face every day regarding race and unconscious bias. It is the multiracial, multicultural faith community that has the potential to set the frame for healing on issues of race and bias. Such experiences are to be seen as part of the process for spiritual growth and practice.

It must also be observed that the process of becoming more inclusive and diverse carries with it unexpected challenges. The following case study demonstrates this.

A Case Study

Presenting Issue

As congregations move toward greater diversity and consider the strategic steps to be taken on this journey, one of those steps may be to diversify the staff. This step is a crucial matter and complex in its dynamics.

In the case of one congregation, their vision and strategic plan set a goal to become more racially and culturally inclusive. This constituted a congregational culture shift that should not be underestimated for its challenges. The strategy included plans to hire an African American associate minister to join the senior minister, a white woman.

The Congregation's Circumstances

1. Alongside this vision were some preexisting tensions, underappreciated for their seriousness—tensions in the congregation between the white senior minister and some members.
2. Complicating the strategy to become more diverse was an ad hoc group of African American members convened by the senior minister to advise her on her own awareness of issues and sensitivities regarding race and culture in the congregation. This group was not tethered nor accountable to the governance structure of the congregation.
3. As the Black Lives Matter movement grew, a group of predominantly white members self-organized and convened to address racial justice issues on behalf of the congregation. This group likewise was not tethered nor accountable to the governance structure of the church. It was reported that some of these members were among those who were dissatisfied with the senior minister.
4. When the African American staff member entered the system, he was asked to meet with and resource the predominantly white Black Lives Matter ad hoc group while the white senior minister met with her ad hoc African American advisory group. While diversifying the staff is one important step in a larger plan to become more inclusive, it is equally important that staff and the congregation have a holistic and strategic plan for becoming more diverse and inclusive. All activities and efforts are then driven by the plan and are coordinated and unified. This also avoids placing too much of the burden for instituting this culture shift on the person of color in their staffing role.

In predominantly white congregations that attempt to diversify ethnically, there can arise unconscious biases and manifestations of racism that reside below the surface in conflict situations. At issue here is the attachment by some to the associate minister of color who held both tangible and symbolic roles in the system. The tangible role was his contribution to the congregation's goal to become more racially inclusive and to give leadership to this end. The more symbolic role was that this person may have represented, for some, the achievement by the congregation to have already become antiracist and inclusive by the mere fact of adding a clergy person of color to the staff. This may account for the high emotional reaction by some to his eventual departure from the staff. Feelings of deep disappointment and anger, even betrayal, surfaced at this point. What felt like a significant turning point for the congregation appeared to be experienced by some as an accomplishment that was snatched away by the "failure" of this situation. Some may have experienced this as a reversal of commitment to the congregation's vision. However, it was the unsuccessful effort by leadership to address the emotional content of this event that did not allow for adequate healing for some.

When the congregation attempting this culture shift is predominantly white and adding an associate-level person of color to the staff—a situation with strong potential for conflict—there are a few questions that are helpful to ask:

1. Do we hold transparent expectations for the role of this staff person? The congregation may expect its vision for a more diverse and inclusive membership to be effected single-handedly by this staff person. It is a manifestation of racial bias to place such expectations upon the person of color to now deliver on the congregation's vision. Without shared

ownership by the congregation and structural support for this effort, there is a high likelihood of failure.

2. Have we done the preparatory work needed to maximize achieving the vision? The leadership of the congregation must first embrace the vision and be conversant on the details of plans to intentionally move the congregation in this direction. Likely this includes changes in worship, adult education, the church's Web site, and some new program initiatives. The structural support needed is in the form of ongoing conversations among members on issues of racial awareness, hospitality, leadership, and power dynamics. It is also important that there is a clear job description with deliverables and timelines for this position and a duly appointed team of members who work with and support this staff person.

3. How will we evaluate this effort and address concerns along the way? It is essential that there is a mechanism for assessing, supporting, and evaluating the process and the work. This effort is on the agenda of every significant organizational component in the life of the congregation. Everyone carries some portion of the vision and reports on the efforts being made in their area of responsibility. Mutual accountability is a high expectation.

4. How do we care for relationships as we seek to realize our vision? As the congregation becomes more diverse, it is of vital importance that members care for one another and the staff. Intentionality in building and supporting the leadership team and asking ourselves "How are we doing?" is key to ensuring creativity and openness.

5. Has this vision been lifted up regularly as the congregation's spiritual calling in worship, on the Web site, in church newsletters, and as part of the stewardship of the congregation? The vision is not an add-on but is at the core of the congregation's identity.

6. Have we anticipated that concerns and issues arising along the way may require the assistance of outside expertise? A mistake often made by congregations generally, but especially in multiracial, multicultural settings, is that they wait too long to access such expertise when a need arises.

Congregations do themselves a great service when they provide training and tools for their leaders in managing conflict and difference before a conflict arises. Training that gives leaders a basic set of skills and awareness of congregational dynamics is vitally important to its health.

ANALYZING CONFLICT

Read aloud the following lists of sources of conflict (outlined in more detail on pp. 71–72) and compounding and contributing factors. How do you see these elements present in the above case study? Do you see any of them present in your own congregation?

Sources of Conflict

1. Core values, conflicting expectations

2. Basic beliefs, ethical framework

3. Power, control, and accountability or lack thereof

4. Resistance to needed change, actions against the best interests of the organization

5. Interpersonal issues/emotional intelligence—behavior patterns, leadership styles, manipulation, attitude of disregard, lack of boundaries

6. Intrapersonal issues—lack of self-awareness, unresolved personal issues, misdirected energy

7. Lack of transparency, hidden motives, subsequent trust issues

8. Institutional issues—governance structure, confusion of roles, allocation of resources

9. Cultural difference, race, class, gender, and sexual orientation issues

Compounding and Contributing Factors

1. The behaviors exhibited in response to the presenting issue can become the central issue.

2. Communication becomes guarded and anxiety driven, accusatory, and lacks transparency.

3. There is sabotage through withholding information, making confidentialities public, remaining silent when someone speaks derogatorily about another and unfairly so.

4. People choose sides, secretly recruiting, pressuring others to support their point of view, and creating unhealthy divisions.

5. There is a lack of stated norms for how conflict will be dealt with in a relationship.

How could the situation in the above case study and in your own congregation be transformed by enforcing the following guidelines for creating a more productive dynamic?

Creating a More Productive Dynamic

1. Speaking to, not about, the person with whom you have an issue.

2. Listening to the other rather than formulating your next argument.

3. Creating norms and safe space for difficult conversations.

4. Being clear about your boundaries and what's nonnegotiable.

5. Being transparent and owning one's own stuff.

Review Stages 3 and 4 of the Pentecost Paradigm

– Have you developed a behavioral covenant for how the congregation will be in community together?

_____

_____

_____

_____

_____

_____

_____

_____

_____

_____

– Have you provided conflict training for congregational leaders?

_____

_____

_____

_____

_____

_____

_____

_____

_____

_____

Chapter 9

Communicating and Organizing

Seven weeks after Passover, our Jewish friends celebrate a feast day known as *Shavuot* (Weeks) in Hebrew and Pentecost in the Greek. *Shavuot* has a double meaning. First, it is the culmination of a season of harvesting grains, which began at Passover and ended at Shavuot (Jer. 5:24; Deut. 16:9–11; Isa. 9:3). Second, it is traditionally a day to celebrate the giving of the law to Moses at Mount Sinai. It's a time to make a pilgrimage to Jerusalem; a time to read Torah and to add greenery to house and temple; and it is a time to eat a wonderful treat, like cheesecake!

Those of us who are Christian celebrate Shavuot/Pentecost as the birthday of the church. Let me remind us that on the Day of Pentecost recorded in Acts 2, many Jews from towns whose names are hard to pronounce had made a pilgrimage to Jerusalem for the holiday. According to Luke (the writer of Acts), 120 believers were gathered there, including the disciples—the eleven plus Matthias, who took Judas's place—following the instructions of Jesus to wait for the gift of Spirit. And the Spirit shows up and shows off: big windstorm and tongues that look like fire landing on each of the disciples, giving them an *amazing* ability to speak languages that they do not know. Luke is very specific when he describes this miracle of communication:

> Parthians, Medes, Elamites, and residents of Mesopotamia, Judea and Cappadocia, Pontus and Asia, Phrygia and Pamphylia, Egypt and the parts of Libya belonging to Cyrene, and visitors from Rome, both Jews and proselytes, Cretans and Arabs—in our own languages we hear them speaking about God's deeds of power. (Acts 2:9–11)

"Deeds of power." What does this mean? In our holy imagination, we believe that multiracial, multicultural gathering of humanity heard the disciples tell stories about God as liberator, God as way-maker, God as healer, heart fixer, justice worker. They heard the disciples testify that in the midst of the horrible oppression at the hands of the Roman Empire, with evidence of the most despicable behavior by the emperor and his cabinet, in the midst of corruption and erosion of human rights, as an assault on the most vulnerable and marginalized, trampling on the souls of the dispossessed in the name of national greatness—those disciples told stories of the dream of God, the reign of God, already in the midst of them, creating heaven on earth.

The disciples told stories of truth, empathy, and resistance. They told stories of God's ability to heal the world. We believe leaders need to be able to *story* God's vision for a healed and whole world, in as many cultural languages as possible, so the people can understand it. Hear it. See it. And see how this vision fits for their lives, how they are part of the vision. This is really important, from our point of view. This is what "evangelical" means to us: telling the good news of God's deeds of power in all of the languages we can, by any means necessary. "Pentecostal" means, to us, in the way of Pentecost, with the primary gift being the gift of varied speech, so that all who listen can hear what God is saying to them: you are mine, you are loved, you are called—get busy!

Rather than have a clergyperson assigned to evangelism, Middle Church created the position for a director of communications and outreach. We believe today's church needs to think of evangelism as a project of communication and of organizing. That project is internal and external. We are storying the vision that God calls us to inside our community, outside our community (to the community we intend to "recruit"), and to those on the border—those who worship online but who have not yet joined us; those who drop out to travel, or because they are busy, or their feelings got hurt (this happens in multiracial, multicultural churches, as it does in all churches).

Some of the writers who have most influenced my (Jacqui's) thinking—Virgilio Elizondo, Gloria Anzualdúa, Donald Winnicott, and W. E. B. Du Bois—have helped me to think about *border spaces* as the containers in which people of different cultures and races converse, connect, and create a new identity. These are the spaces that segregationists fear, because we *will* change on the border. Our identities are not as solid; we become more fluid and embrace the parts of ourselves that are like the other. The stories of those around us deeply impact our own story. On the border, we are both this and that; border spaces are not so much about either/or, but rather about both/and.

On the border, the way we speak changes; we use some of the vocabulary and syntax of our neighbors in our own speech. Working with Black Lives Matter activists has changed my vocabulary. In my activism with the LGBTQ communities, I have a new patois. In the border space, I am straight, black, female, married, middle-aged, *and* multiracial. I have also been queered in my theology, in solidarity with my LGBTQ family. As I plan worship, as a leader, I need to *speak* classical music, gospel music, Broadway music, and spirituals. When I preach, teach, and pray, I need illustrations, anecdotes, and other signals that all are welcome to the table of fellowship and all belong inside the story of God's grace.

Since multiracial, multicultural congregations are border spaces, what kind of communication skills do we need? How can we communicate to the broad diversity of peoples both in our congregations *and* outside our doors, to whom we are also called? Leaders on the border must develop unique communication skills, *multivocal* communication skills, so they can help followers see how they are cast in the great drama of human beings joining the divine to heal souls and heal the world. In other words, *we need to speak in many tongues.*

By "speak in tongues," I mean that we need the following tools and tactics in order to communicate.

Using Simultaneous Discourse

Communication on the border requires language that affirms the people in the congregation—their experience, their journeys, their courage to be on the border, their hopes, dreams, and their fears—storying the goodness of this choice. And at the same time, often in the same newsletter, sermon, or prayer, leaders have to use language that contests and critiques injustice, hegemony, and discrimination. This is the both/and language of the prophets. On the one hand, can you see that God is with us, doing a bold new thing in us, using us in the service of healing? On the other hand, let me lament with you how broken our world is, how painful it is, and how much it can feel that God is absent or not present enough. Leaders on the border in multiracial congregations have to speak truth to power on the one hand (prophetic speech) and comfort God's people in an experimental border space on the other (pastoral speech).

What does this look like? Let me give you one example. The morning prayer at Middle Church is our prayer of intercession, our prayers of the people. We had a guest preacher on Pride Sunday in 2017, and so it was my job to pray that prayer. Pride Sunday is such an upbeat day. The music is lively, often pulled from both sacred and secular texts. We used a little R&B about celebrating good times, some pop music that describes a woman's journey to her own voice. Before the sermon, a beautiful anthem acknowledged God's love for all of us. The hymns evoked confidence in God's love for all humanity. After my prayer, one choir was scheduled to sing a text that put God in every breath we take. Along with all the joy in the room, there was grief over terrible events: the anniversaries of the murders at Pulse nightclub in Orlando and the murders at Mother Emmanuel in Charleston; the fact that though Philando Castile had been killed by a police officer and died from his wounds, the officer was found "not guilty." The terror wreaked on transgender women of color. A Muslim teenaged girl murdered while on the way home from mosque. These and other losses swirled amid the joy. In this particular prayer, I set up the both/and nature of the day. Much to celebrate, much to mourn, and that God is present for all of it. I put us in the liminal space of a healing world that is not yet healed. People were deeply moved by the gravity and serious naming of the sorrow, the grief, the specificity in naming painful experiences, and the strong affirmation of our community and our God.

Using Cultural Competencies

Leaders on the border have to communicate with cultural competence. We might learn this by making mistakes, but learn we must. We are not only communicating in both prophetic and pastoral speech; we must also communicate in the cultural languages of the people in our congregation and those we wish to reach. W. E. B. Du Bois's seminal text *The Souls of Black Folk* (1903) inspires me to think about the ways leaders on the border have to develop many cultures inside themselves. He called this "double consciousness" when referring to the ways African Americans survived by holding both their blackness and the consciousness of whiteness inside themselves. Virgilio Elizondo's thinking is similar as he writes about how cultures on the border are *mestizaje* (mixed). I think leaders in multiracial, multicultural congregations need to have consciousness of many cultures as they communicate. This means communicating with intention. How will this hit the ears and hearts of the various cultures represented in my congregation? Where might I need to redouble in my messaging, in order to have my message received by that seventy-something biracial, single woman and that thirty-something biracial couple with two babies? How can I use other bodies and other voices to make sure we are culturally appropriate so that the message can be appropriated?

Middle Church has been committed to being a multiracial, multicultural, fully inclusive congregation since 1985, under the leadership of my predecessor, Gordon Dragt. We work for justice 365 days a year at the intersections of racial, economic, and gender/sexual orientation. As a womanist, I know that these issues are inextricably connected. In our space Middle Church holds racial/ethnic diversity, genders/gender performance diversity, and sexual orientations. It is a brave space in which we also work to create safe-enough space for us to celebrate each other and wrestle at the places where wrestling should happen because we are different.

We worked on marriage equality at the New York State level and at the federal level. I was with my congregation and a sea of straight and queer people, celebrating at the historic Stonewall Inn the day marriage equality became law in the United States of America.

As I write this, I know that the word "queer" is both empowering to many LGBTQ people and offensive to some. Today, many of the young adults in my circles use the word "queer" to describe themselves; they eschew the LGBTQI initialism that they might have chosen before and the labels they represent. Still, about four years ago, influenced by conversations both with young adults and in academic circles, I used the word "queer" for the first time in the pulpit, citing queer theology as a resource for my sermon. One man in his late thirties was deeply offended by this. He had been bullied for most of his life for being gay. I understood from my conversation with him that he would never accept this word, just as I will never accept the word "nigger."

I tucked that word away and asked my staff to do the same. I dropped back, meeting with that young man and many other gay, lesbian, bisexual, and transgender people in my congregation. While meeting in one-on-ones, I was listening, like an ethnographer, for how they described themselves over time, for what language they used to describe their joys and sorrows, their feelings of marginalization and inclusion. I became a student, not just of the textbooks on my shelves, but also of the living texts in my congregation. By deepening my relationships with the people in my congregation, I increased my vocabulary for prayers and sermons, for e-blasts and blogs. Though I am straight, I became a student of these cultures in such a way as to grow my competencies. And I learned how and when to use "queer" and when not to. Communicating God's radical love to as many people as we can, honoring their culture, is a competency for leadership in multiracial, multicultural settings.

Consider another example, this one about the importance of communication as we organized Middle Church for the Black Lives Matter movement: Though we had been committed to multiracial, multicultural, intentional community for three decades, the context of American life shifted around us. The election of Barack Hussein Obama caused some parts of America to claim a postracial reality and others to bring their racism and homophobia out of hiding. The onslaught of murders of black people at the hands of law enforcement reached epic proportions. From Michael Brown to Eric Garner to Tanisha Anderson to twelve-year-old Tamir Rice to seven-year-old Aiyana Stanley-Jones—black people lost their lives in encounters with police officers. Choked to death on a sidewalk, shot in the back, shot while sitting in an automobile, shot while sleeping on a sofa, shot while playing with a toy gun, shot while standing on a corner—their lives were cut short, and in too many cases to stomach, the police officers were not held accountable for these murders.

As Black Lives Matter gained prominence, some of my congregation resisted. "How can we say Black Lives Matter? Don't we think all lives matter?" These criticisms went to some on the consistory (our board) and to some of the staff. The leadership defended me, saying, "This is Jacqui's calling; we must understand her particular passion." This did not satisfy me. To me, the Black Lives Matter movement was *our* calling, not just mine; this call was a logical and theological extension of our call to be a multiracial, multicultural congregation, a manifestation of our call to be antiracist.

I took the criticism as an opportunity to teach. I realized that I was taking for granted that Middle Church understood the Black Lives Matter movement, that they were clear about why the movement existed and what it purposed to do. I took for granted that my preaching was enough background to bring them along with me, and I was wrong, so I dropped back. I took a little time off from preaching Black Lives Matter and did two things. First, I preached our vision instead. I reminded us of our identity and our history. I reminded us that we are the church that opened our arms to folk who were dying with HIV/AIDS, offering comfort, a hot meal, support, and spaces for grieving those who had died. I reminded us that while 11:00 o'clock on Sunday is the most segregated hour for many American congregations, that is not true for us. I reminded us that we celebrate culture and heritage and ethnicity as part of our love of God and neighbor. I preached about our work on marriage equality, both at the state level and the national level. And I reminded us of why we march down Fifth Avenue every Pride Sunday.

Second, I supplemented what I was doing in worship and preaching with adult education conversations and with one-on-ones. I met with those who were most concerned (including my Chinese friend Gloria) to see what their questions were. Then we started a class called "Erasing Racism," in which we used Scripture and books to take racism on directly. This class flourished so much that folks who wanted to go deeper asked for more. So we started a Healing Racism Task Force, a closed group of thirty-five people who would meet for a year to learn each other's stories and to talk about how racism impacts all of us.

With these classes as a context, I circled back to do some expository sermons on race. I came to understand that it was important to help Middle Church hear more than "Black Lives Matter" whenever it was said. And so we began to speak of Black Lives Matter as the last phrase of a paragraph that went something like this:

> When black lives matter, when black children live as long as their white counterparts; when black mortality rates, HIV infection rates, and incarceration rates are more in line with statistics for white people; when the wealth gap between whites and blacks is reduced to zero; when voting rights are not eroded; when law enforcement officers are indicted for killing black people, then black lives will truly matter. Because black people are among the "least of these" in these United States, when Black Lives Matter, all lives will matter.

We also had to connect the dots from what was once a hashtag to the very real stories of the men, women, and children murdered and their families and the sense of terror sweeping our nation.

In one instance, Alesia Thomas was arrested at her home on suspicion of child endangerment after she left her children at a police station because she couldn't care for them. According to a video of the arrest, while putting a handcuffed Thomas in a squad car, Officer Mary O'Callaghan hit Thomas in the throat with an open hand, threatened to "punt" Thomas in the genitals, and then did so—seven times—hitting her in the groin, abdomen, and thigh. O'Callaghan is seen laughing and smoking a cigarette while watching Thomas struggle in the backseat of the squad car. Thomas is heard saying, "I can't . . . move, I can't breathe . . ."; she died shortly afterward at a hospital. O'Callaghan pleaded not guilty to an assault charge in Thomas's death in 2013. In June 2015 she was convicted of "assault under color of authority" and sentenced to thirty-six months in prison, with twenty months of her sentence suspended.

I share the details of this one story, because stories actually do change the story. Although we wrestled with language, we did not wrestle with the narrative. The accumulation of the accounts of these stories in the American narrative put lumps in the throats of my Middle congregation and kindled fire in our hearts to do something about it. We had to keep these stories before the community, and not only those stories, but also stories of poverty, of the rescinding of voting rights, and the very real and present danger to black trans-women in our nations' cities. These stories are intersectional, with racism and white supremacy being the tie that binds them together. We had to connect those stories, weaving them together as the context in which our gifts for ministry are required. Our challenge was to help Middle Church see the narrative of racism as one counter to the narrative of the reign of God. Further, our opportunity was to help Middle people see themselves as partners with God in the healing of our nation

Using more words with care and patience, and weaving together the national narrative, the historical narrative, and the narrative of the dream of God—all this helped my congregation to see that the gay rights movement and the movement for Black Lives are part of our work in civil rights, part of our call to implement the reign of God here on earth.

Tips for Care-full Communication

1. Be a radical listener: hear what is really being said, not what you presume the speaker is saying.
2. If appropriate, repeat for clarity: "What I hear you saying is . . . Did I get that right?"
3. Stay present, rather than rehearsing the point you are going to make.
4. Give good eye contact, facial cues, and body language that signal your willingness to hear.
5. Speak for yourself, from your own point of view. You are not the spokesperson for others in your group, either in the room or outside of the room.
6. Use "I" statements as often as possible. "When I'm . . . When I . . . I think that I . . . I feel that I . . . My concern is . . ." Follow those with how something affects you rather than an observation about the listener. "When I'm interrupted, I feel . . ."
7. Leave space for others to speak, and invite those who are quiet to participate. Pay special attention to signals from people of color that they may be disengaging. Most people of color expect white people to dominate conversations. If you want to change this norm, you need to be intentional.
8. Do not interrupt!
9. Develop your "border" sensibility. Read books and magazine articles that put you in the shoes of the "other." Listen to music that brings other cultures into your soul.
10. Cultivate a relationship with a friend on the border. Break bread together, coach one another, and hold one another accountable. Empathic communication is the fruit of these relationships. (See more about work on the border in chapter 10.)

Using Many Media and Modes

Our Director of Communications and Outreach, Christina Fleming, says that the first minister people often meet at Middle Church is our Web site. Many visitors find Middle Church by searching for "gay friendly," "progressive," or "gospel music." Christina, our communications team, and I understand that today effective evangelism uses many forms of media. The team listens closely to what is being planned in worship and in our activism and programming, which we organize in our three areas: LGBTQI and gender justice, disrupting racism and white supremacy, and economic justice. They help create strategies for sharing that information in many media, including our weekly e-blast, our monthly mailed newsletter, our Web site, our Facebook pages, our Twitter and Instagram accounts, our YouTube Channel, our sermon and worship podcasts, and our live-streamed worship celebration.

Let's consider worship as an example. Our worship is spectacular—spiritually moving, rich with arts, with many voices participating. Still, worship itself is not likely to be newsworthy. Although our worship team plans worship six months to a year in advance, we make space for the breaking news to shift what we do. When events happen around the globe—natural disasters, tragic violence spawned by xenophobia, one more death at the hands of police, or events on the global political theater—our congregation expects us to say something about it and give them a way to do something about it. Our favorite journalists often need personal, local stories about how individuals and communities respond organically to the most current news; we invite them into worship, and we tell our stories (this is evangelism on the down-low!). Thus our worship, justice, and communications teams collaborate to (1) plan what we sometimes call an *ethical spectacle* to highlight the current issue in worship; (2) alert journalists of our plans and invite them to worship with us; and/or (3) prepare a video clip or photos and publish them in the world of the Internet and social media.

Our decision to wear hoodies during worship before George Zimmerman was arrested and after he was acquitted for the killing of Trayvon Martin was mentioned in dozens of news stories across many major news outlets. Likewise, thousands of people saw our message of celebration when we performed a triple gay wedding during our morning worship celebration after the gay marriage bill passed in New York State in 2011. Three hundred people saw the wedding in worship, but almost five thousand people have seen the thirty-minute YouTube video. (Links to all these stories can be found at middlechurch.org.)

Here are other examples regarding our commitment to economic justice. Our Butterfly Meal program makes six thousand sandwiches a season for hungry people at two local parks. We partner with the Micah Institute, promoting a $20-per-hour living wage. We housed the activists of Occupy Wall Street after they were evicted from Zuccotti Park, and our Gospel Choir and I participated in a telethon to raise money for a related program, intended to relieve debt. The choir sang a spiritual, "Woke Up This Morning with My Mind on Freedom," and I spoke on the biblical concept of jubilee—when all debts are pardoned and the poor are liberated from bondage. MSNBC's *Up with Chris Hayes* featured our work; this is an example of the ways partnering with the media can help amplify messages of justice.

I am sure that part of what put Middle Church on MSNBC's radar was our willingness to be with the press and to invite them to be with us. I had the great honor of joining Melissa Harris-Perry as she covered the fiftieth anniversary of the Selma to Montgomery March. I've had televised conversations with Joy Reid, Chris Hayes, Rev. Al Sharpton, and others as we tackle current events. For a short season, I had a show at MSNBC.com called *Just Faith*, where we had edgy conversations about faith and politics.

Your local news stations might be a place to start in terms of getting in front of cameras to share the story of God at work in your context. Be sure to imagine with your team and with people in your congregation who might be journalists or activists: What kind of content is faithful to who we are, relevant to others, and newsworthy at the same time? Creating your own media is an easier first step to take.

For example, we were so outraged at the Sandy Hook shootings. We took a vanload of people to D.C. to join a protest. But we also generated our own ethical spectacle. With the help of RAWtools, we melted down and repurposed a gun into a farming tool during worship, acting out what both Micah and Isaiah write about turning "swords into plowshares" to stand up for gun violence prevention after Sandy Hook. We collaborated with the Groundswell Movement at Auburn Seminary to create a petition, and I wrote a blog at Huffington Post.[1]

Submitting op-ed columns to media outlets is an important way religious leaders can communicate their stories. We recommend training through the Op-Ed Project or media training through Auburn Media, so you gain the tools for your story to be heard in our sound-bite culture. Whether it's a Web site, a blog, or a local TV story, beginning with a personal narrative opens the heart. Policy and legislation does not move people, but stories shift our minds and culture.

Partnerships amplify our voice. Through Auburn Seminary and the Groundswell Movement, sixty thousand people were e-mailed about the national Gun Violence Prevention Sabbath, and our online viewing audience tripled that Sunday. (For more about partnerships and collaboration, see chapter 10.) When you are planning or have completed an event, share the details with your social justice partners—your media contacts—with language and images they can use in social media.

Community Organizing 101

Through all of our communication tools, our aim is to change the story, to communicate the importance of addressing racial justice inside our congregation and in the larger community. At Middle Church, we think that larger community is our congregation-in-waiting; our parish is the city of New York, the nation, and any people around the globe who might come and visit us when in Manhattan or find us online. We are recruiting people to a worldview, inviting them to join the love revolution, which we think can dismantle racism and heal our nation.

Even though our ambition is to build a movement for Revolutionary Love that is global, we understand that our work begins with local organizing. Part of our communication strategy means getting ready for the new world we will inhabit, with norms that allow for increased racial and cultural diversity. This requires intentionality about shifting our culture; the way we are is as important as what we do. We used the exercise below to examine the norms in our system; it will work in yours as well.

NAMING AND SHIFTING NORMS

A Process for Staff, Board, and Key Leaders

1. What are the stated norms in our system? What are the implicit ones?

2. What is the theology undergirding the norms?

3. How do these norms enable multiracial and multicultural connecting?

4. How do these norms impinge or inhibit this connecting?

5. List the new norms that need to be in place in order for a multiracial, multicultural community to grow and thrive.

6. Brainstorm what you need to do to get the norms in place.

7. What norms do we need in order to affirm the racial/ethnic, cultural, gender, and sexual diversity on our team?

8. What norms need to be in place in order for us to achieve our five-year vision?

9. What norms need to be in place in order to affirm our commitment to racial/ethnic, gender/sexuality, and economic diversity?

10. What behavioral covenant can we write to express these norms? How can we communicate this covenant to our congregation?

As we mentioned in the chapters on change and conflict, this border work that creating multiracial, multicultural congregations requires will inevitably lead to resistance and conflict. This makes communicating with tenderness and clarity essential. Even congregations enthusiastic about this new direction will experience some sense of loss of the way things used to be. Having new people from different ethnic and cultural backgrounds in the congregation necessarily means new norms and shifts in power. Creating a container for these changes means carefully communicating care for those doing the work. We hope you find these tips to be helpful in your context. Regardless as to your stage in the Pentecost Paradigm, communication is a mission-critical skill.

Review Stages 3 and 4 of the Pentecost Paradigm

– What are the ways you tell the congregation's story internally to the members?

_____

_____

_____

_____

– How are you telling this story to the larger community?

_____

_____

_____

– Are leaders living into new roles, and has the organizational structure and the congregation's budget been aligned to reflect who and what it is now?

_____

_____

_____

– Are members of the congregation still telling one another their stories?

_____

_____

_____

_____

Chapter 10

Collaborating in the Public Square

I (Jacqui) grew up in the Protestant Church. My congregational experience began in a quaint, white clapboard church on Pease Air Force Base in Portsmouth, New Hampshire. In that context, as a little girl, I thought church meant the fifty or sixty people worshiping with us on any given Sunday morning. This was our experience on a base in Michigan as well.

As a teen in Chicago, I served as an elder at the Seventh Presbyterian Church. I had the opportunity to work closely with my pastor and five adults to think about mission and vision for our small congregation. Most importantly, I realized that we were connected to other congregations in the presbytery of our city, other churches in our region, and other churches in the nation through our annual General Assembly. These connections also extended to One Great Hour of Sharing, an international agency supporting children and families with food and clean water; to Caesar Chavez's organizing of farm workers; to incarcerated men and women in Cook County Jail; and to the Heifer Project, which provided livestock to poor families in developing countries. I caught a vision that the church was larger than me, than our small congregation, and even than our denomination. I came to understand that we had a mission to do, which included sending kids to camp, making sure everyone had enough resources and food on the table. Church meant making sure everybody was all right!

I graduated from Princeton Theological Seminary in May 1992. That summer, I had the great opportunity to do a Ten-Day Training with our local Industrial Areas Foundation organization. The community organizing principles that I learned enhanced my understanding that as a clergyperson, my parish is my community, my city, my nation, and the globe. It became crystal clear to me that if people of faith are called to combat the powers and principalities that oppress the people of God, we need to harness not only our shared dreams but also our collective power. This power is best gained as we collaborate together in the public square.

On the way to my ordination that November as Minister of Word and Sacrament in the Presbyterian Church (U.S.A.), I remember conversations with mentors about being a pastor, priest, and prophet in my ministry. I think these are three modes of operation that often happen simultaneously, like the discourse I described when speaking about multivocality. Sometimes in the same sermon, I am shepherding and holding my congregation while I articulate a prophetic critique or vision of a preferred reality. And then I will pray as a priest, offering sacraments that point to God's grace. Thinking about three modes of ministry makes it simpler to imagine that I am less local congregational minister and more pastor, priest, and prophet to a nation.

My parish includes that Muslim family, frightened at escalating anti-Muslim sentiment, and those Jews at our partner synagogue, who are working on ending mass incarceration. My parish includes the mother worried about a raid from ICE; the queer teen in Idaho, who is looking for a way to come out; that young man whose brother committed suicide after being released from jail; and that brilliant professor, a lonely senior woman with a big heart and a small apartment. My parish includes those two guys who saw me on Joy Reid's *AM Joy*, came to Middle Church, and joined three weeks later. It also includes those people tracking me in social media, some who agree with me, and some who don't.

How do we respond to all of our "congregation," those who have joined our movement and belong to our church and those who are out there, needing to know that our God calls us to love, period? We can't do this by ourselves. We are best called, I believe, to do our soul- and world-healing work in partnerships that leap the bounds of denominations, religion, race, and ethnicity.

Theology in Public

First, let me say, Jesus was a public theologian. Yes, he spent time in temple, but most of what is recorded about his ministry happened outside. Second, Jesus was political. He was embroiled in a theological, *political* battle with corrupt religious authorities of his own faith and with Rome; a battle about the interests of the people. Third, Jesus understood the power of a good story (parables) and an *ethical spectacle* (curse the fig tree, turn the tables upside down, feed the five thousand on the mountaintop). Finally, Jesus was the theologian-in-residence of his movement. So, if we are Christian, or if we are inspired by the teachings of Jesus, then we are in good stead when we go public about our faith and ethics, when we are political (being about the people, the polis, the whole society), and when we are willing to enact an ethical spectacle on behalf of the reign of God. This is what it means to be a public theologian: we do God-talk out loud.

I am so blessed that my job description includes the phrase "public theology." All of us who preach, teach, and write for congregations—clergy and lay leaders alike—we are generating theology for public consumption. The things we write and speak go out into the world in the hearts and minds of our congregants. One Sunday I preached a sermon about making sure Middle Church is a "safe container" for us to change, grow, and be transformed. I was thrilled when Meghan and Tynisha, two of our moms, shared this story with me. "We were listening to Elijah play in her room with her toys, and we heard her say, 'It's OK, baby, the container is safe here!'" Elijah is three years old. I am sure she heard me say that, but I imagine she heard her Mommy T. and Mommy M. talk about worship and overheard them quoting me as well. We are, all of us, being quoted and paraphrased as the Word goes forth. Songs from worship play in the heads of congregants, accompanied by snippets of sermons, prayers and art that comforted them or challenged them.

Right after the election of Donald Trump, our congregation was mostly in a state of shock and disappointment. Many of our members are gay, and they worried about changes in legislation that might hurt them. I married Marvin and Vaughn, and they wondered if their marriage was in jeopardy. Our elders worry about Social Security, our young adults about health care. All of us are deeply concerned about the uncivil discourse in the public square.

The day after the election, a bunch of us—Muslims, Christians, Buddhists, Sikhs, and Jews—gathered in Washington Square Park to hold each other, to sing, and to pray. These were partners, among them Auburn Theological Seminary, Lab Shul, Judson Memorial

Church, and the Arab American Association; and then there were partners of partners. We started small, maybe a hundred people. Soon students from New York University and The New School joined us. We were a web of humanity, drawn together by the loss of a shared dream. We lifted up our voices, we held hands. We said short prayers from all of our traditions. We *had church,* as my people would say, right out there in public. Many photos were snapped and shared in social media. Our theology of "love is love" was literally being shaped out of doors and then echoed in social media.

Many were preparing for a trip home at Thanksgiving, and they wondered how to talk to relatives about the election. Some felt betrayed by their loved ones who pulled the lever for Mr. Trump. In a sermon, I generated some questions for "care-fronting" loved ones and encouraged Middle folk to tweet about how it went. Twitter is a great partner in the public square. I understand now that it is a fast-moving river for short conversations. If I dive in quickly and engage the people there, Twitter becomes a conversation tool to relate to my congregation and also the virtual congregation that is waiting to join our movement. Here are some ways we do theology out loud at Middle Church:

- We manage two Facebook accounts, one representing the congregation and one representing me as pastor. Our team shares content on both, strategically.
- We manage two Instagram accounts, one for me and one for the congregation.
- We manage three Twitter accounts, one for me, one for the congregation, and one for our partner, The Middle Project. (The Middle Project is our partner 501(c)3 that prepares ethical leaders for a more just society.)
- We manage three Web sites, middlechurch.org, middleproject.org, and jacquijlewis.com. These sites help people find our unique voice in the public square. Almost every Sunday there are people at our church from Europe, most often from France! We have somehow found our way to a Web site there, recommended as a destination for gospel music and a joyful worship celebration in New York City.
- I blog as often as I can for Huffington Post Religion, Patheos and Auburn Voices. These blogs sometimes draw people to the congregation, and they almost always drive people to my Twitter account. This is usually good news, though sometimes my universalist, progressive points of view get me into hot water. I am not as churchy as some other Christian clergy.
- I say "yes" often when invited to speak in the public square, accepting opportunities to grow our virtual church followers. As a Senior Fellow at Auburn Theological Seminary, I am part of a network of interfaith leaders working for justice across this nation. I have joined my friends Bishop Dr. William Barber II, Linda Sarsour, Sister Simone Campbell, Brian McLaren and Rev. Michael-Ray Mathews to speak at rallies about voting rights, mass incarceration, and health care. These relationships are so important; they are a ready-made space of collaboration and support. Rabbi Sharon Brous and I had a chance to appear together on *The TODAY Show.* John and I had the opportunity to appear on HBO's *VICE News* on a special about *Loving v. Virginia* and interracial love. And when I had my show *Just Faith* on MSNBC.com, the Auburn Fellows kept me in talent! Speaking at rallies, graduations, and lectures leads to new friends and partners; opening our congregation for the media builds strong partnerships. People find us online, and sometimes they come to visit at church! I always schedule myself to preach the first Sunday in July. Why? Because there are always new people at church, people who have seen us march along Fifth Avenue on Pride Sunday.

- I am sometimes invited to speak on national news shows, and I accept the invitations whenever possible. Doing a good job—being clear, warm, present, and playing well with other guests—gets me invited back. Though I am fearless in the pulpit, I used to be terrified of the camera, self-conscious, and awkward. My friends at Auburn Seminary—especially my buddy Macky Alston—offer a fantastic media training. Check them out at auburnseminary.org.

Tips for Doing "Theology Out Loud" in Your Context

- As we discussed in the previous chapter on effective communication, make good use of multiple forms of media:
  - Social media tools like Twitter, Facebook, and Instagram are free; they offer you a platform to shape any way you want to. Consistent posts in your own voice are effective.
  - Make use of hashtags—#LoveLooksLikeThis or something similar. Create your own buzz by asking congregants and community members to participate.
  - Build relationships with your local paper. Ask to offer op-eds or a regular column on faith in public life.
  - Build relationships with your local affiliate of a major network. Take the religion or political reporter to coffee. Offer to be available for stories that touch on faith and politics.
- Attend the graduations of your local colleges and high schools. Seek invitations to speak at the ceremony and at moments of other rites of passage.
- Form a lectionary study group or, even better, invite your favorite rabbi and imam to be in a study group with you.
- Look up your local Black Lives Matter chapter and offer to bring food for the leaders at the next meeting. Ask how you can help.
- Invite elected officials from each major party to come to your house of worship and talk about the issues.
- Participate in marches and demonstrations that align with your vision for a just, inclusive, and compassionate society.

Marchin' and Dyin' In

In search of truth and justice, I have marched with the most amazing people I know, surrounded by a horde of others. There is something very powerful about praying with your feet. We marched in New York City for Black Lives Matter—more than once; we marched for justice for Michael Brown and Eric Garner. We marched for the rights of women in D.C. We marched against gun violence in D.C. as well. We marched to give a moral agenda to Hillary Clinton and Donald Trump when they were running for president. We marched against Islamophobia. We marched in Selma for the fiftieth anniversary, and we marched at Mother Emanuel in Charleston after nine souls were slain. We marched in horror at the murders at Pulse nightclub in Orlando. We marched for Marriage Equality. We marched to stop an assault on health care; some of us (me included!) were arrested as we stood up for the rights of God's people to have affordable health care. There is a palpable power in the hum and din of people chanting, marching, talking, praying, singing. Marching for a just cause is a moving sermon.

The purpose of an ethical spectacle is that it captures the attention and the imaginations of those who are watching. All around the globe, men, women, and children marched for the rights of women right after the election of Mr. Trump. All around the globe "Hands up, don't shoot" became shorthand for the predicament of unarmed Michael Brown, slain at the hands of a police officer in Ferguson, Missouri. And "I can't breathe," the terrible cry for help uttered by Eric Garner before he died, was repeated in marches and in die-ins all over the globe as well.

You may not feel you are in a context to enact these ethical spectacles. One of my colleagues, a white clergywoman in Missouri, says she felt unauthentic doing a die-in. But she enlisted her congregation in a neighborhood watch program. As white liberal people of faith, she felt they could authentically stand watch, in solidarity, while their colleagues of color protested. My clergy friends and I have sometimes made a circle around young activists, giving them cover with our collars as a way to keep their interactions with the police safe.

Learning Communities

There are many conferences and learning opportunities at which you can increase your own capacities and connect with other organizations and leaders who share your values. Every year since 2007, Middle Church has offered a conference for leaders in multiracial congregations. The Leading Edge Conference brought together the best thought leaders to talk about creating worship, doing justice, and training leaders how to be in the border space of multiracial, multicultural life. In recent years, we rebranded our conference Revolutionary Love and went straight at the problems of race in America. Thought leaders like Van Jones, William Barber, Serene Jones, Ebony Turman Marshall, Brian McLaren, Zainab Salbi, and Valarie Kaur have been on faculty, with some 400 people in residence and as many as 55,000 watching online at some point. Attendees form learning circles of support that extend beyond their time together in New York.

Sojourners has offered The Summit—a learning/leading opportunity—each June for a few years. The Wild Goose Festival is a gathering of artists and activists inspired by Spirit to heal the world. Brian McLaren, The Center for Progressive Renewal, and Convergence are creating a seminary without walls and a continuing education curriculum for clergy and lay leaders. The Right Rev. Gene Robinson has assumed the role of Vice President and Senior Pastor at the Chautauqua Institution, providing executive leadership for the Department of Religion and chairing a new volunteer advisory group on faith in society. Repairers of the Breach provides national training and policy development under the leadership of William Barber. Auburn Theological Seminary offers training not only in media but also in leadership and movement building. And Sr. Simone Campbell and NETWORK are pushing for policy change and offer educational resources on policy and advocacy developments.

This year our little people were invited into a learning community called The Interfaith Playdate. The imam at our local masjid was concerned about his children, in light of a rash of anti-Islamic violent events. He invited the children in all of the communities who have been in an interfaith relationship for about a decade to come and play at the masjid. The playdate is a powerful, mobile learning community; each partner takes a turn hosting. We are Muslim, Christian, Jewish, Hare Krishna, and Buddhist. Music, games, and lessons on each faith tradition are surrounded by laughter, pizza, and ice cream.

Work on the Border

Ideas for Collaboration in Your Community and Context

Our work in the public square begins with our passion for creating a more just, multiracial, multicultural, radically loving world. And we must be equipped with resources—which includes wisdom, tools, and colleagues—in order to do the work we are called to do.

No matter what, the border calls you. You may not live in a large city as I do, but no matter where you find yourself, the dream of God is calling us to create communities that are multiracial and multicultural. This work requires us to collaborate in the public square. It requires us to work on the border. Here are some practical things to put in place as you complete God's dream.

- *Find a learning community.* Make time for continuing education. Read everything you can. Look up the authors in the index of this book and read them!
- *Investigate.* Engage in a weekend of ministry by exploring your community. Who are partners in your community with whom you can do social justice work? Is there a school, a food pantry, a nonprofit that can extend your ministry reach? Invite the leader to a one-on-one conversation and ask the now-familiar Vision questions: *If vision is the picture of a preferred reality, what do you see in five years? What does your organization look like? What does our community look like?* Find the places where your vision and their vision intersect. Plan to meet again when each of you will bring a colleague to see what they might cook up for joint programming or a focus on justice.
- *Create work and play opportunities.* Build a partnership with a congregation near you that is of a different race/ethnicity, religion, or faith group. Have teens and young adults join in an "Art Creating Life" event. Have your youth groups do a service project together. Send your young adults to have coffee together to see what they might cook up for joint programming.
- *Study and worship.* Worship with another congregation that dreams of a multiracial, multicultural future. Plan worship together and switch pulpits. Form a joint reading/discussion group, and study my sermon booklet, *For the Healing of the Nations.*[1] Engage in Bible study with your boards and key leaders.
- *Engage young adults in interreligious learning experiences.* Invite those aged twenty to forty to bring friends who are from other faith traditions or are non-affiliated to a recruiting party. Enlist faculty mentors from your congregation to teach them about managing money, community organizing, getting the careers they want, and using social networking to change the world.

- *Plan a Seder.* Connect with your local synagogue during the spring holy days. Think about how to use gospel music and klezmer music to surround an Agape Meal/Seder celebration on Maundy Thursday. Write a haggadah with your rabbi colleague that focuses on liberation and justice.
- *Plan to honor the Eid al-Fitr (end of Ramadan) feast with your local imam.* Using PBS resources, offer to host an intergenerational celebrative meal and a conversation on Muslims in America.
- *Create opportunities to worship across faiths.* Invite your imam and rabbi to lead worship with you on Martin Luther King Day, and then make it a quarterly ritual.
- *Make space in your building for partnerships.* Invite the local AA, NA, and Al-Anon chapters to meet in your space. Create a partnership with other congregations to offer food, clothing, social work support, and job training to your community. Open your space to artists for rehearsals, auditions, and the creation of art. They can repay you by participating in worship or teaching a class.

In concluding this chapter, I want to say a word about Rabbi *Yeshua* (Jesus). When dealing with the corruption of religion and the evil of empire, Jesus was asked to reduce the gospel to a sound bite. (This is my holy imagination at work; he was asked about the most important commandment.) He told his followers to love God with everything we have and love our neighbor as we love our selves. In other words, *Love.* Period. When calling for revolution, Jesus spoke of love.

I look around our nation and around the globe with clear-eyed criticism of religious systems. Too many of us are failing our people and failing the God who calls us into ministry. We are keepers of the status quo. We bless greed and oppression because we do not articulate how they break the backs of the people and the heart of God. And we are too often content to stay in segregated silos, where people talk like us, walk like us, look like us, and think like us. How poor is the church that won't celebrate the richness of God's diverse creation? How small is our imagination if we think God is only speaking our language and only has room for our kind in the reign of God?

Jesus was a revolutionary, calling for reform. The kind of revolution he espoused is a love revolution. Love that speaks truth to power. Love that stands up for the poor and marginalized. Love ensuring that everyone has enough. Do you want that revolution? Do you want a revolution?

John and I write this book calling for revolutionary love as a force to heal racism, white supremacy, and xenophobia. We write this book believing that congregations that can celebrate racial/ethnic and cultural diversity can heal the American heart and can overcome the stubborn plague of racism clogging the arteries of our land. We feel this work is urgent and that we need partners in order to do it. We are convinced that this revolutionary love must be enacted in the public square, so that it can be witnessed and duplicated. We write, fingers flying on the keys, for the urgency of *now*.

Review Stages 4 and 5 of the Pentecost Paradigm.

– In your context, what do you see as opportunities to bring the message of love and reconciliation to the public square?

_____

_____

_____

_____

_____

_____

– How might collaborating with a partner or partners increase your impact and theirs?

_____

_____

_____

_____

_____

_____

– Identify your local media outlets and create a strategy for engagement with the public.

_____

_____

_____

_____

_____

_____

Conclusion

*M*any whites cannot comprehend the notion of *white privilege*; they deny that they enjoy certain benefits and freedoms not afforded people of color. In fact, many claim they do not feel privileged in any way. They look at their lives and feel that they have not received payment on the promise of the American Dream. These are the folks who are underemployed, without job security, or lacking decent health care. Their children are deeply in debt with educational loans or could not afford college in the first place; they may not have the prospect of doing better in life than their parents. In their view the very concept of *white privilege* is a cruel assertion. It is a conundrum that the circumstances of these white people are very much the same as so many people of color, yet a great gulf has existed between them since slavery and the structure of plantation economics. How would all their lives be better if common cause were forged between them?

However, even crueler and more absurd to these whites is the notion of reparations for the generations of slavery and Jim Crow oppression of African Americans, a form of oppression that not only disadvantaged a whole population economically and socially, but, as some argue, has poisoned the very psyche of black people.

Sitting alongside these concepts of white privilege and reparations is a mostly sincere desire by many white people to effect reconciliation between the races. Jennifer Harvey, in her book *Dear White Christians*, has stirred controversy by asserting that we will never achieve the goal of racial reconciliation in this country until we come to terms with the issue of reparations. She maintains that white people aspire to "make everything all right" through reconciliation without the necessary conversation and action needed to repair the generations of damage done to African Americans. It is our experience that many whites react to this premise angrily and with little tolerance. Their reaction is formed by their belief that they cannot be held responsible for what happened so long ago.

It is in this context that we now find ourselves dealing with demands for "white affirmative action" as whites feel they have been wronged by every attempt to balance the scales of justice. Many whites sense that they pay a direct price for and are diminished by every action that levels the playing field for people of color. It is a characteristic of white privilege that white people do not need to know nor want to know the true story of suffering and degradation visited upon black people shackled by hereditary chattel slavery. Snatched from their homeland, enslaved Africans were an imprisoned and imported labor force that physically cleared the land and built this nation, some learning to read and write illegally beyond the view of their white overseers.

Now is the time for people of faith of all races, ethnicities, and cultures to sit at the table together and struggle our way through the historically calculated, manufactured, and divisive structure of race and break down the dividing walls of hostility. This work will be challenging, but it will, we believe, heal the soul of our nation. We believe multiracial, multicultural congregations that welcome and include all of God's children have a unique role to play in disrupting racism, white supremacy, and fear of the stranger.

We also believe that this is holy and ethical work. Every year, Middle Church offers a conference to train and network leaders committed to this work of dismantling racism. We believe racism is *the* twenty-first-century problem in the United States of America, and the church must lead the way to the love revolution that will disrupt its corrosive power. We welcome you as colleagues and allies in this struggle. Our God is in the business of liberation; let's join her!

Notes

INTRODUCTION

1. Robert P. Jones, *The End of White Christian America* (New York: Simon & Shuster, 2016), 1.
2. Curtiss Paul DeYoung et al., *United by Faith: The Multiracial Congregation as an Answer to the Problem of Race* (Oxford: Oxford University Press, 2003), 2.
3. Ta-Nehisi Coates, *Between the World and Me* (New York: Random House, 2015).
4. *Crash*, written and directed by Paul Haggis, available as DVD (Santa Monica, CA: Lions Gate Entertainment, 2004).

CHAPTER 1: EMBRACING CALL AND COMMITMENT

1. Martin Luther King Jr., *Letter from a Birmingham City Jail* (April 16, 1963), https://www.africa.upenn.edu/Articles_Gen/Letter_Birmingham.html.
2. Ibid.
3. Parker J. Palmer, "Leading from Within: Reflections on Spirituality and Leadership," in *Let Your Life Speak: Listening for the Voice of Vocation* (San Francisco: John Wiley & Sons, Inc., 2000), 78.
4. Walter Brueggemann, *The Prophetic Imagination*, 2nd ed. (Minneapolis: Fortress Press, 2001), 13.
5. Ibid., 69.
6. Dennis Jacobsen, *Doing Justice* (Minneapolis: Fortress Press, 2001), 15.
7. Thandeka, *Learning to Be White: Money, Race, and God in America* (New York: Continuum, 1999; New York: Bloomsbury, 2013).

CHAPTER 2: CASTING THE VISION

1. Lovett Weems, *Church Leadership: Vision, Team, Culture, Integrity* (Nashville: Abingdon Press, 2010).
2. Alice Mann and Gilbert Randle, *Holy Conversations: Strategic Planning as a Spiritual Practice for Congregations* (Bethesda, MD: Alban Institute, 2003).
3. Jacqueline J. Lewis, *The Power of Stories: A Guide for Leading Multiracial and Multicultural Congregations* (Nashville: Abingdon Press, 2008).

CHAPTER 5: BUILDING CAPACITY

1. Daniel Goleman, Richard E. Boyatzis, Annie McKee, and Arthur Morey, *Primal Leadership: Realizing the Power of Emotional Intelligence*, eAudiobook (New York: Macmillan Audio, 2002).
2. Parker J. Palmer, "Leading from Within," in *Let Your Life Speak: Listening for the Voice of Vocation* (San Francisco: John Wiley & Sons, Inc., 2000), 78–91.
3. Michael Brown was shot by a police officer on August 9, 2014, in Ferguson, Missouri, leading to massive protests.

CHAPTER 6: CULTIVATING COMMUNITY

1. DeYoung et al., *United by Faith*.
2. Thomas Jefferson, *Notes on the State of Virginia* (New York: Penguin Classics, 1998).

3. Jacqueline Janette Lewis, *Authoring Stories for the New Religious Frontier: A Theo-Ethical Narrative Analysis of Clergy Serving Multiracial/Multicultural Congregations* (PhD diss., Drew University, 2004).

4. D. W. Winnicott, *Playing and Reality* (London: Routledge Classics, 1995).

5. Ronald A Heifetz, *Leadership without Easy Answers* (Cambridge, MA: Harvard University Press, 1994).

6. Howard Gardner, *Leading Minds* (New York: Basic Books, 1995), 14.

7. Ibid.

CHAPTER 7: CELEBRATING IN WORSHIP

1. You can find the video of this piece, and so much wonderful music from all of our choirs, on the Middle Church YouTube channel, https://www.youtube.com/channel/UCAIdHUDuBF6lrl56FoYdMrA.

CHAPTER 8: UNDERSTANDING CONGREGATIONAL CONFLICT

1. Speed Leas, *Moving Your Church through Conflict* (Bethesda, MD: The Alban Institute, 1986).

CHAPTER 9: COMMUNICATING AND ORGANIZING

1. Jacqueline J. Lewis, "Honoring King by Turning Guns into Plowshares—Literally," *Huffington Post*, January 20, 2014, http://www.huffingtonpost.com/the-rev-jacqueline-j-lewis-phd/guns-into-plowshares_b_4630004.html.

CHAPTER 10: COLLABORATING IN THE PUBLIC SQUARE

1. Jacqueline J. Lewis, *For the Healing of the Nations: Sermons on American Racism* (New York, Middle Church Books, 2018).

CPSIA information can be obtained
at www.ICGtesting.com
Printed in the USA
FFHW010542210219
50612646-55971FF